# THE GOSHEN FACTOR

## MOVING INTO THE CURSE FREE ZONE

# THE GOSHEN FACTOR

## MOVING INTO THE CURSE FREE ZONE

John Parish

*Goshen Factor: Moving Into The Curse Free Zone*
ISBN: 978-0-88144-206-9
Copyright © 2010 by John Parish

Published by
Thorncrown Publishing
9731 East 54th Street
Tulsa, OK 74146
www.yorkshirepublishing.com

# Contents

# CHAPTER 1

# GOSHEN LIVING IN AN EGYPTIAN WORLD

## (BLESSED IN A CURSED WORLD)

Gen 45:10-11

*And thou shalt dwell in the land of Goshen, and thou shalt be near unto me, thou, and thy children, and thy children's children, and thy flocks, and thy herds, and all that thou hast: And there will I nourish thee . . .*

There is a vital issue that the people of God must confront until the Coming of the Lord. It is the question of how we are to survive until the promised trumpet sounds and the command is given to come up higher.

There are specific passages in the Scriptures which graphically portray prevailing conditions of the Endtime. Jesus stated that the mayhem which existed in Noah's day would surface again and dominate the culture.

He also signaled the conditions of Sodom as a fitting comparison to Endtime trends.

Luke 17:28-29

*Likewise as was in the days of Lot, they did eat, they drank, they bought, they sold, they planted, they builded. But the same day that Lot went out of Sodom it rained fire and brimstone from heaven, and destroyed them all. Even thus shall it be in the day when the Son of man is revealed.*

This passage presents a picture of Endtime society. It reveals Last Day culture, and even depicts economic factors. The Lord underscored that a preoccupation with material concerns would go hand in hand with debasing immorality. The prophetic Word accurately projected global, societal, military, and even moral patterns. When it comes to how believers are to react to the perils of this unique prophetic hour, the Word of God showcases the deliverance of the Hebrews from Egypt as a model of our soon exodus from this judgment-bound world.

The Apostle Paul defined the mindset and activities which constitute "perilous times" in his second letter to Timothy. After describing the moral and spiritual devastation of satan's last day assault, he wrote the spirit of Egypt would assert itself again.

Just as in ancient Egypt, the culture will experience an explosion of knowledge and technology, but depraved minds can never properly appreciate the facts which they've discovered.

2 Timothy 3:7-8 (King James Version)

*Ever learning, and never able to come to the knowledge of the truth. Now as Jannes and Jambres withstood Moses, so do these resist the truth: men of corrupt minds, reprobate concerning the Faith."*

Jannes and Jambres were Pharoah's magicians. They counterfeited the first three miracles of Moses and then discovered the limits of satanic power. They mimicked Moses by appearing to turn their rods into serpents, but Moses' rod swallowed their fabricated miracle. They could turn water into blood on a small scale; in contrast the God of Moses turned the entire Nile into a river of blood. They could duplicate the plague of frogs, but couldn't stop the misery that it caused. Pharaoh was compelled to implore Moses to call off the frogs.

When it came to changing dust into lice, the magicians had exhausted their demonic energy. Only the true God can change dust. He created man from dust, promised to make Abraham's seed as numerous as the dust, made dust to burn on Elijah's altar, and announced that one day the dust in the grave of His redeemed people will sing when their resurrected bodies burst forth in eternal triumph.

The only thing the devil can do with dust is choke on it. The Hebrew word for serpent actually means the "dust eater". The Scripture repeatedly refers to satan as the "old serpent", the "old dust eater." Perhaps the greatest reason that Jesus instructed His disciples to shake the dust off their feet when they were ill treated, was to turn the tide against our adversary. The only way the serpent can be silenced is to gag him with the dust of sorrow and frustration which he thought to put on us. Through the power of Jesus' Name, we can overturn the strategies of the Wicked One.

Those believers who appropriate the promise to "tread on serpents" cause our arch-enemy severe indigestion when we refuse to let the difficulty of the moment destroy our faith, nullify our joy, or silence our praise.

Pharaoh's magicians had to admit that when dust became lice to afflict their idolatrous land, it was nothing less than "the finger of God." If the Lord follows the Exodus pattern of mass deliverance today, then we can expect satan's Endtime agents to soon come to the limits of their ability. When the enemies of righteousness behold the superior power of our God in signs, wonders, and miracles, they will realize what the Lord can do with something as trivial as dust.

The enemies of the Gospel are about to witness a demonstration of "the finger of God."

The Psalmist said, "For he knoweth our frame; he remembers that we are dust." (Ps. 103:14) Despite the culture's defamation of committed believers, the finger of God will anoint the dust of human frailty to defeat the works of darkness. Soon our enemies will have to admit that the Greater One abides in us. (Deut. 32:31)

In these days we can expect the Lord to continue His age-old pattern of using the foolish things of the world to confound the wise.

## THE SPIRIT OF EGYPT IS RESPONSIBLE FOR THE ESCALATION OF DEMONIC ACTIVITY

I Timothy 4:1 (King James Version)

*Now the Spirit speaketh expressly that in the latter times some shall depart from the faith, giving heed to seducing spirits and doctrines of devils."*

The Last Days will witness an exponential increase of devilish power. This unprecedented demonic activity is aimed at destroying humanity's conscience and blurring the distinction between good and evil. The Apostle Paul reveals the objective of demonic spirits is to promote lies of hypocrisy which sear the conscience.

The spirit of Egypt will be responsible for enormous pressure and stress in the Last Days. There will be nothing like it in the annals of history.

Jesus warned of the cares of this life, men's hearts failing them for fear, wars, rumors of wars, pestilence, and earthquakes.

4

The upheaval will take its toll. Hatred of the Faith will reach new levels. Persecution of Christians in the recent past has been largely confined to Communist and Islamic countries. But given the increased hostility toward Bible believers in America, it may not be long until real Christians experience an all out assault. Jesus said, "They shall lay their hands on you, and persecute you, delivering you up to the synagogues, and into prisons, being brought before kings and rulers for my Name's sake." (Luke 21:12)

Luke 21:16 (King James Version)

*And ye shall be betrayed both by parents, and brethren, and kinsfolk, and friends; and some of you shall they cause to be put to death.*

The spirit of Egypt will instigate widespread betrayal. The Name of the Lord will be so despised that we who claim and worship Him as the only Savior will become the victims of politically correct hatred. God's response to this pervasive iniquity is to position the globe for seven years of unprecedented travail. Undiluted judgment will be poured out.

Matt 24:21-22 (King James Version)

*For then shall be great tribulation, such as was not since the beginning of the world to this time, no, nor ever shall be. And except those days should be shortened, there should no flesh be saved: but for the elect's sake those days shall be shortened.*

The powers of the upper atmosphere shall be shaken. The entire planet will become unsteady and its normal rotation cycle disturbed. The weight of man's sin will cause the globe to sway on its axis. The delicate infrastructure of earth's ecosystem will be disrupted.

Isaiah 24:19-21 (King James Version)

*The earth is utterly broken down, the earth is clean dissolved, the earth is moved exceedingly. The earth shall reel to and fro like a drunkard, and shall be removed like a cottage; and the transgression thereof shall be heavy upon it; and it shall fall, and not rise again.*

The Word of God foretells coming catastrophes to do more than inform us of future events. The Holy Spirit included this information in the Scripture so that God's people would not be unduly alarmed when these events begin to come to come pass. We have the promise that "God has not appointed us to wrath, but to obtain salvation by our Lord Jesus Christ." ( I Thess. 5:9 King James Version)

The promise of a sudden catching away of the church is a clear word from the Lord. (I Thes. 4:16) No one who *rightly divides* the Scripture can honestly dispute the promise of His Return (I Cor. 15: 52) The theological gymnastics of pseudo clergymen cannot alter the truth that God is planning to rapture His Church in the not-to-distant future.

Rev. 3:10 (King James Version)

*Because thou hast kept the word of my patience, I also will **keep thee from** the hour of temptation, which shall come upon all the world, to try them that dwell upon the earth.*

The wording of the Master's promise is precise and specific. He did not say that He would take us *through* or *out of* the hour of temptation, but keep the believer *from* it. The "hour of temptation" is a reference to a specific period of time which try those who are attached to this world. A close examination of the passage reveals that Jesus is speaking about the prophesied seven years of Tribulation revealed in Daniel 9:27. The Apostle John recorded a chronological description of those years in Revelation chapters six through nineteen.

No doctrine of the New Testament is assailed any more than the promise of a pre-Tribulation rapture. This promise is the first to be compromised and the first to be abandoned by those who seek a modified Christianity. False brethren who are fond of the pleasures and carnal lifestyles of this world loath the prospect that God may soon call His church home.

Fanciful theories are currently promoted which suggest that God has cancelled the Rapture for lack of interest. Eschatology professors are now advancing a notion that all prophecies of a coming Tribulation can be avoided. The Church is under tremendous pressure to adopt a more politically correct version of the Endtimes.

Seminaries are teaching their ministerial students that we can have the Kingdom without the King. Not a few voices are gaining popularity with their teaching that once the church has been relieved of its Biblical baggage, a new day of utopian unity will dawn with a new world government and one world religion.

These are just some of the lies spoken in hypocrisy. The denial of the Rapture is a part of the strong delusion which Paul warned about in II Thess. 2:11. A Rapture-less Gospel is a travesty and danger that will mislead multitudes into accepting the proposed solutions of a false church. It is advocated by those who seek to redefine the status and mission of the Body of Christ.

There is a paradigm shift in the ministry. Instead of calling the unsaved from the broad way of destruction to walk the narrow path of eternal life, a host of "pseudo apostles and deceitful workers" are seeking common ground with false religions and ideologies. They are substituting environmental causes and social justice issues for the Gospel. Reprehensible agents of satan are wrapping themselves in clerical robes and pretending to be ministers of righteousness. (2 Cor. 11:15) A Gospel that denies the imminent Return of the Lord Jesus is not the Gospel of God.

The promise of Revelation 3:10 echoes the Lord's statement made from the Mount of Olives:

Luke 21:36 (King James Version)

*Watch ye therefore, and pray always, that ye may be accounted worthy **to escape all** these things that shall come to pass, and to stand before the Son of man.*

Beneath all the promises of our ultimate deliverance is the question of what we do in the mean time. How do we handle the pressure?

What do we do about the trend to depart from the Faith? How do we survive the onslaught of "seducing spirits and doctrines of devils?" How do we overcome when we must simultaneously face spiritual, physical, mental, and financial pressure? How do we deal with problems that are overwhelming and stress that is all too often overpowering?

The Word of God contains divine directives for overcoming the immense challenges of these times. Amid the many instructions which teach the believer to *occupy till He comes* is a depiction of our deliverance. The Hebrews in Egypt is a picture of the redeemed of the Lord in this present day world. Egypt always appears in the Scripture to represent the world's system and ideology. Egypt is called *the house of bondage and rebellion.*

Isa 30:1-2 (King James Version)

*Woe to the rebellious children, saith the LORD, that take counsel, but not of me; and that cover with a covering, but not of my spirit, that they may add sin to sin: **That walk to go down into Egypt,***

*and have not asked at my mouth; to strengthen*
*themselves in the strength of Pharaoh, and to trust*
*in the shadow of Egypt!*

Egypt was the center of world idolatry, perversion, and abomination. It was warlike, materialistic, and boasted that it was an advanced civilization. The Egyptians studied the arts, invented mathematics, and originated many of the sciences.

They participated in grotesque methods of worship to their false gods. Repeatedly, the Lord told the patriarchs to "go not down into Egypt." The sons of Jacob sold their brother Joseph to Midianites who subjected him to slavery in Egypt. It is where he suffered, was falsely accused, and imprisoned. However, it was also where he was exalted to become lord of the entire land and master of its resources.

The famine in the land of Canaan was so severe that Jacob sent his sons to purchase food in Egypt. It seems strange that famine could happen in the Promised Land. But this, too, is a picture of Endtime conditions. Not all the Last Day famines are agricultural. One of the most serious famines is happening in today's church even though believers are surrounded by relative material abundance.

Amos 8:11-12 (King James Version)

*Behold, the days come, saith the Lord GOD, that*
*I will send a famine in the land, not a famine of*
*bread, nor a thirst for water, but of hearing the*
*words of the LORD: And they shall wander from*
*sea to sea, and from the north even to the east, they*
*shall run to and fro to seek the word of the LORD,*
*and shall not find it.*

This prophecy doesn't need any elaboration. Here in America it is evident that the preaching of the true Gospel is a rare event. The Word of God has been replaced with motivational lectures and self-esteem teachings. So called *seeker-friendly* churches have opted to compromise the Word of God and accommodate the culture to increase their attendance.

Recently, mega-churches have come into existence, owing their phenomenal attendance to market research. The leaders take great pains to foster a casual night-club atmosphere. Darkened auditoriums, strobe lights, and music patterned after rock groups convey the idea that any lifestyle is now acceptable to God.

There is no preacher, no pastor, and no minister at these new mega gatherings. All Biblical authority is held in contempt and disdained by a generation that has lost respect for holy things. The leaders of these new churches prefer to be known as life coaches. They are usually dressed in a Hawaiian shirt, cut off shorts, and flip flops proclaiming to the audience that they are an agent of change. Every truth of the Scripture is either repudiated or redefined. The crowd is told that sin is no longer sin, there are no absolutes, and all religious roads led to the same place. The new message of these contemporary churches is *don't worry, be happy, and life is just a party.*

This famine of hearing *the words of the Lord* is the result of cultural - accommodating trends in the ministry. The conventional wisdom is that the preaching of the Cross, the necessity of the born again experience, the empowering of the Holy Ghost, the Scriptural demands for a separated life, and the promise of the Lord's Return has become obsolete and offensive to this generation's tastes and philosophies.

So the church is assimilated into the godless culture around it. People who truly hunger for the Presence of the Lord are left to diligently search for some place where the reality of His power and truth is boldly proclaimed.

Just as the prophet Amos foretold, the believer is forced to hunt in these days for someone with a true Word from God. But there is a place divinely preserved and prepared for those who hunger and thirst for righteousness.

There is a spiritual reality where its occupants are exempt from the famine of the End Times. It is not a fantasyland or an ethereal sphere of altered consciousness. It is not geographic as it was in ancient times, but is today an atmosphere where the mighty presence of God creates an environment where believers are supremely blessed. It is a place in God where the Spirit of the Lord orders our life, controls our circumstances, and implements the divine promises.

It is an oasis in a desolate desert of despair. It is an island in an ocean of worry and fear.

It is a place of refuge from Endtime storms. It is a rock that can't be shaken when the whole world is collapsing. This spiritual state of *life and life more abundantly* can only be described as *Endtime Goshen*.

**Those in despair over present world conditions need to take a fresh look at the model of our deliverance depicted by the Hebrews in ancient Egypt.**

Joseph, a type of Christ, recognized that He was in Egypt to use his position and resources to prepare a place for the covenant people in time of famine. The place that Joseph chose for the seed of Abraham was called *Goshen*.

Goshen was located in the extreme northeast corner of Egypt. It was pasture land and suitable for the unique needs of Jacob's tribe. It was different from the rest of Egypt. The Hebrews could still follow the ways of the Lord and not mix with the Egyptians as long as they dwelt in Goshen. Egyptian idolatry and lifestyle would have no influence over them as long as they stayed in their designated area.

Goshen was a good place to wait for the ultimate return to the land of Canaan.

Joseph understood the necessity of Goshen to shelter and sustain the children of Israel, but the dangers of Egypt pressed heavily on his father's mind. Famine required movement, but Egypt was less than an ideal choice. In the night season, the Lord spoke a prophetic word to Jacob.

Genesis 46:3-4 (King James Version)

*And he said, I am God, the God of thy father: fear not to go down into Egypt; for I will there make of thee a great nation:*

*I will go down with thee into Egypt; and I will also surely bring thee up again: and Joseph shall put his hand upon thine eyes.*

Jacob was unaware of God's plan in preparing Goshen as an intermediate place to rescue his people from famine. If the Lord led them into Egypt, then it was to bless and prepare his descendants for the day when they would return and totally possess the land. The Lord would surely bring them up again. His purpose would not be altered or changed by famine or even by their sojourn into a foreign environment. Somewhere in Egypt, God would provide and protect His people until the time to possess their inheritance arrived.

All God's future plans for the seed of Abraham would become clear to Jacob when Joseph's hands were laid on his eyes. The touch of God's advance-man in Egypt meant more than insight into the future. It imparted a revelation of God's divine provision for the present.

Such a revelation awaits the believer who makes contact with Heaven's advance-man in the world today. The Holy Spirit is present and active to *enlighten* our eyes of understanding that we *may know what is the hope of His calling* and experience *the riches of the glory of His inheritance in the saints.* (Eph 3:18 King James Version)

The revelation which Jacob received in his visitation demonstrates the faith of Abraham. This is the faith that the Holy Spirit imparts to every believer in Christ. (Gal. 3:9 King James Version) It is the supernatural assurance that even when we encounter rough times, difficulties, and unexplainable hardships, the Lord will never abandon us to our surroundings.

We are facing a spiritual, financial, mental, and emotional Egypt in these Last Days. The times are fraught with peril and danger. The future is menacing. The world is sinking into an economic morass never seen before. The culture is beyond depravity and is exceeding the immorality of Sodom. Living in this present world is indeed a fearful prospect, but the word spoken to Jacob is not limited to him alone. The promise that God will sustain His people through hard times, and ultimately lead His redeemed to the ordained inheritance is timeless. It is a word for us today.

Jacob didn't know it at that time, but God had a purpose for Egypt. His descendants would become a great nation while they sojourned there. His children would be mightily blessed in a place that was antagonistic to every thing he believed. They would come out by a series of miracles, and leave the land with great wealth and riches. In spite of famine and an evil culture, the children of Israel would be blessed, preserved, and delivered.

This is not just good history, but good news for God's people living in these perilous times. The believer must understand that the promises of the Lord are designed to shape our reality, especially in times like these. Surrounded by proponents of political correctness, daily attacks on the Word of God that malign the Name of the Lord, encircled by fear of a collapsing economy, facing the spectre of an emerging global government, bracketed by naysayers and doomsday scenarios, we will, nevertheless, *prosper and be in good health as our soul prospers.*

Bad times do not negate the promises of God. His Word does not depend on the vagaries of the stock market. His promises are not conditioned on cultural trends. "Let God be true, and every man a liar." The projections and prognostications of the pundits will fail, but we have a more *sure word of prophecy.*

Long ago, our God placed *handfuls on purpose* for His people in these times just as Boaz did for Ruth. He has a meal barrel that can't be emptied and a cruse of oil that never fails. He can still put a coin in a fish's mouth. He can still multiply fish and bread for the hungry. He can command the ravens to bring meals to his prophets, and when the brook that supplies the water dries up, He has another plan ready to keep his servants alive in famine. Isaac will not be the last of God's servants to reap a hundred fold in the year of famine. The Lord is capable of doing it again for those in a covenant relationship with Him.

Every Bible student is aware that Jesus is preparing us a place in Heaven, but it should be understood that until our assignment is finished, He has a place for us on earth. The atmosphere and environment of Goshen is being re-created by the Holy Spirit to provide a sustaining place for God's people in the midst of a cursed world. The Hebrew translation of the word "Goshen" means *the place of drawing near.* Our only hope of survival, and increased blessings from the Lord is to draw near to His Presence.

According to Gen. 47:6-- Goshen is the *best of the land.* Egyptians rejected it because this region was suited to pasturing. The Egyptians could not recognize the potential of Goshen because they did not have the mindset of the sons of Israel. Shepherding was the lifestyle of the Hebrews, but *"every shepherd is an abomination to the Egyptians"* (Gen 46:34 King James Version)

The tension between the Christian lifestyle and the world still exists. The world mocks, rejects, disputes and ridicules us. They regard us as an *abomination* to their politically correct ideology, but this will not stop the favor of God from coming to those who are "drawing near" to Him.

Gen. 47:24 (King James Version)

*And Israel dwelt in the land of Egypt, in the country of Goshen; and they had possessions, therein, and grew, and multiplied exceedingly.*

Endtime believers can expect the same treatment from Heaven when we seek first the Kingdom of God and His righteousness.

## There was trouble when Israel ventured out of Goshen.

Goshen was the safety zone for the Israelites. To leave this land into Egypt-proper was an invitation to disaster. Venturing into Egypt made the Israelites vulnerable to the decadence of a condemned culture. Sadly, the alluring temptation to experiment with the pleasures of Egypt proved to be overpowering. In Egypt, the Israelites were in danger of losing their identity and forgetting that they were the chosen people.

The sad fact of our times is that so many believers are leaving the safety-zone of a sanctified and separated life to flirt with the seductions of a condemned world. It is time to rediscover some forgotten Scriptures.

2 Cor 6:17-18 (King James Version)

*Wherefore come out from among them, and be ye separate, saith the Lord, and touch not the unclean thing; and I will receive you. And will be a Father unto you, and ye shall be my sons and daughters, saith the Lord Almighty.*

**15**

1 John 2:15-17 (King James Version)

*Love not the world, neither the things that are in the world. If any man love the world, the love of the Father is not in him.*

*For all that is in the world, the lust of the flesh, and the lust of the eyes, and the pride of life, is not of the Father, but is of the world.*

*And the world passeth away, and the lust thereof: but he that doeth the will of God abideth for ever.*

1 Cor 6:20 (King James Version)

*Having therefore these promises, dearly beloved, let us cleanse ourselves from all filthiness of the flesh and spirit, perfecting holiness in the fear of God.*

We ignore these warnings and admonitions at our own peril.

The occupants of God's Endtime Goshen know that they must keep themselves at a safe distance from Egypt. The blessings depend on it. The promised protection depends on it. The future deliverance depends on it. There is a border that God has established between righteousness and unrighteousness which must never be crossed.

**When it was time for the promised deliverance and return to the Patriarchal Land, there** *"arose up a new king over Egypt, which knew not Joseph."* (Exodus 1:8 King James Version)

The ascent of the new pharaoh is significant because it mirrors present political conditions. The Hebrew phrase for *new king* is "melek chaadash" which means a new type of king. The history of Egypt reveals that a revolution erupted resulting in a change of dynasties. The policies, traditions, heritage, allegiances, priorities, and values of the old dynasty were discarded.

The attitude about God's covenant people was especially changed. Instead of regarding them as an ally and a positive influence on the nation, the new king looked upon them as an enemy. The Hebrews were regarded as a threat to the political objectives of the new regime. They were stereotyped as obstructionists to the new polices which were changing the country. The new king was afraid of their growing numbers and pursued an ambitious program of oppression toward the Hebrews. The goal was to progressively phase them out by cancelling their freedom and destroying their children.

The new king implemented a policy of forced abortions. It was actually infanticide. Every male child was to be killed at birth. *"But the midwives feared God, and did not as the king of Egypt commanded them, but saved the men children alive."* (Exodus 1:17 King James Version)

The new king made life miserable for the Hebrews with hard bondage until a cry went up to the God of Abraham to send deliverance. The phrase which reads the new Pharaoh *"knew not Joseph"* does not mean that he wasn't aware of Joseph's existence or his role in history, but he did not value the contributions which Joseph made to the nation. All of Joseph's philosophy and viewpoints of government were repudiated.

Joseph had been one of the most outstanding prime ministers of Egypt. He spared the nation from a world-wide famine with his God-given wisdom. Egypt experienced one of its greatest periods of territorial expansion under Joseph. The nation never converted to Joseph's God, but had tremendous respect for the God of

**17**

Abraham who gave Joseph the wisdom to govern properly and spare them from the calamity which befell the rest of the world. This new king was blasphemously unthankful that Joseph's God spared the country from global catastrophe.

The parallels with Egypt's changing dynasty and the changes in the political realities of our nation are striking. We have a new king in America. Demonic philosophies through their human agents now rule the land and guide the culture. Biblical concepts of morality are no longer the foundation of our laws. The Christian values and principles of our founding fathers have been cast aside. The moral restraints necessary to continue a free civilization have been systematically removed until *evil is now called good and good evil.* (Isaiah 5:20)

The hostility toward Christians is approaching the level of hatred that was directed toward the Jews in Nazi Germany. With the passage of such laws as the so-called "Hate Crimes Bill", the freedom to preach the entire Word of God is now threatened, and the God-haters have gained legal justification for *"despising those that are good."* (II Timothy 3:3)

The power brokers which govern our country are admitted Communists, Socialists, Marxists, and Globalists. The Chinese dictator, Mao Tse Tung, who slaughtered 70 million of his own people, is openly admired by these new policy makers. Their attitude toward believers is the same as Egypt's new pharaoh toward the Hebrews. We are now regarded as the enemy.

One document from the Department of Homeland Security notified law enforcement agencies that Christians, who believe in Bible prophecy, are to be regarded as potential terrorists. However, it is Muslim extremists who continually plot to blow up planes, detonate car bombs, shoot army recruiters, and go on killing sprees at our military installations. Nevertheless, it is not politically correct to identify Islam with terrorism. So the real enemies are given a pass while new pressure is brought against Bible Christians.

Every believer who is even remotely acquainted with Bible prophecy should read the signs. The time of our deliverance must be near. Shouldn't there be a cry made by God's covenant people at this critical hour for the Lord to come quickly? The time of our departure surely is at hand.

The sins of Egypt, the attitude of their leaders, their grotesque idolatry, their oppressive policies toward the Israelites, and their murderous program of population control resulted in ten plagues on the land. The economy of Egypt was wrecked by these plagues. Their society and civilization were devastated. Egypt lost its war with the God of Abraham just as surely as America will lose its war against Jesus.

**It must be noted that each plague was directed against a certain idol of the Egyptians**.

Turning water into blood was against the Nile god, Osiris.

The plague of frogs was against the frog goddess, Heka.

The plague of lice was against the earth god, Leb.

The plague of flies was against the beetle god, Kopara.

The murrain was against the cattle god, Apis.

The plague of boils was against the goddess Noit.

The plague of hail was against the air god, Isis.

The plague of locusts was against the insect god, Separais.

The darkness was against the sun god, Ra.

The death of the firstborn was directed against Pharaoh himself who claimed to be a living deity.

**19**

**Before Israel's deliverance, they witnessed the Lord execute judgment on all the gods of Egypt.**

Ex 12:12 (*King James Version*)

*For I will pass through the land of Egypt this night, and will smite all the firstborn in the land of Egypt, both man and beast; and against all the gods of Egypt I will execute judgment: I am the LORD.*

Everything the Egyptians worshipped and trusted was exposed as false and powerless. We are witnessing the Lord execute judgment on the false gods which are worshipped by modern idolaters. Egyptian earth worship has made a comeback in the form of radical environmentalism. Snails, whales, reptiles, birds, and other species are believed to be more important than people.

"Earth Day" is the newest holiday recognizing the planet as some sort of deity. It is expected that all will bow down and worship Mother Earth. However, God is executing judgment against the nature worshippers. Notice that the object of their worship is in upheaval.

The globe is rocked by an unexplained wave of killer earthquakes, volcanic eruptions, tsunamis, floods, droughts, solar wind storms that can disrupt the earth's power grids, the disappearance of honey bees which are essential to the world's food supply, bizarre weather, climate change and host of other calamities. There are a prophetic signs in all these natural disasters, but the central message is that the Creator is the only one worthy of worship, not the creation.

Judgment is also being executed on the world's financial structure. The dire predictions from the world's leading economists are enough to make the heart of non-believers *fail for fear, and for looking after those those things which are coming on the earth.* We daily hear the words *economic meltdown,* financial *down turn,* and *market crash.* It is not just industry, banks, and global corporations that are faltering. Entire nations are teetering on the brink. An apprehensive public has been numbed by the word *crisis.* According to the Scripture, the time will arrive when the world's economic system will collapse in one day. (Rev. 18) Money and material things have become the object of worship for multitudes, but judgments are now appearing against these false gods. They can't deliver; they can't satisfy; and they won't last.

Judgment is also falling on society's god of sensual pleasure. A few years ago there were only two sexually transmitted diseases, but now there are close to 40. The dreaded AIDS virus shows no signs of abating and all efforts at finding a cure have failed. There were a few times when laboratory scientists were confident that a vaccine was forthcoming, then the virus mutated and all their efforts were in vain. For some reason, this educated, refined, and technologically astute generation can't connect the dots and understand that *"the wages of sin is death."* (Romans 6:23 King James Version) In case no one has noticed, the idol of sensual pleasure is collapsing.

**All of Egypt was plagued by the judgments directed against false gods, but the dreaded plagues that devastated the land could not cross the border into Goshen.**

Ex 8:22-23 (King James Version)

*And I will sever in that day the land of Goshen, in which my people dwell, that no swarms of flies shall be there; to the end thou mayest know that I am the LORD in the midst of the earth.*

**21**

Exodus 9:4 (King James Version)

*And the LORD shall sever between the cattle of Israel and the cattle of Egypt: and there shall nothing die of all that is the children's of Israel.*

*Only in the land of Goshen, where the children of Israel were, was there no hail.*

*And Moses stretched forth his hand toward heaven; and there was a thick darkness in all the land of Egypt three days:*

*They saw not one another, neither rose any from his place for three days: but all the children of Israel had light in their dwellings.*

*But against any of the children of Israel shall not a dog move his tongue, against man or beast: that ye may know how that the LORD doth put a difference between the Egyptians and Israel*

Our Lord revealed Himself as the Judge of Egypt and simultaneously the Savior of His convenant people.

The border of Goshen is where every plague stopped because it was the temporary residence of Abraham's seed.

1 Corinthians 10:11 (King James Version)

*Now all these things happened unto them for ensamples: and they are written for our admonition, upon whom the ends of the world are come.*

Just as God made Goshen off-limits to every plague, He has promised to preserve and prosper His people in this present world until He calls us to meet Him in the air.

**22**

Ps 91:10 (King James Version)

*There shall no evil befall thee, neither shall any plague come nigh thy dwelling.*

Psalm 32:7 (King James Version)

*Thou art my hiding place; thou shalt preserve me from trouble; thou shalt compass me about with songs of deliverance. Selah.*

Psalm 27:5 (King James Version)

*For in the time of trouble he shall hide me in his pavilion: in the secret of his tabernacle shall he hide me; he shall set me up upon a rock.*

After Jesus enumerated Endtime calamities, He said, "but not a hair of your head shall perish." (Luke 21:18)

In every section of the Scriptures, the Holy Ghost reveals a spiritual dimension where the covenant people are sheltered from the awesome trouble of the world. Proverbs is one of the major wisdom books of the Bible. Divine revelation was imparted to Solomon so that we could understand how to overcome, endure, triumph, and avoid the trouble in troublesome times.

Proverbs 3:25-26 (King James Version)

*Be not afraid of sudden fear, neither of the desolation of the wicked, when it cometh.*

*For the LORD shall be thy confidence, and shall keep thy foot from being taken.*

The Pauline epistles consistently reveal that God will preserve His people in dangerous times.

2 Timothy 4:18 (King James Version)

*And the Lord shall deliver me from every evil work, and will preserve me unto his heavenly kingdom: to whom be glory for ever and ever. Amen.*

2 Timothy 1:12 (King James Version)

*For the which cause I also suffer these things: nevertheless I am not ashamed: for I know whom I have believed, and am persuaded that he is able to keep that which I have committed unto him against that day.*

The Lord revealed that divine preservation is offered to those who truly commit their life to Him.

Luke 17:33 (King James Version)

*Whosoever shall seek to save his life shall lose it; and whosoever shall lose his life shall preserve it.*

Through faith in His promises, obedience to the Word, and separation from ungodly lifestyles, the born again believer can dwell in a corner of this world which can only be described as Goshen.

Goshen is where the plagues can't touch us. It is where the grievous troubles of the world cannot invade. It is where we prosper in the midst of perilous times. It is where we are blessed even though surrounded by devastation and destruction.

I pray that those who read this book will leave Egypt with all of its sinful pleasures, idolatry, warped concepts of reality, twisted emotions, philosophical absurdities, and corrupted lifestyles to dwell in Goshen.

Years ago, I heard the late famed radio commentator, Paul Harvey, talk about Mr. Kerr during the horrendous

San Francisco earthquake of 1906. Mr. Kerr produced the famed canning jar still in existence to this day.

His glass factory in San Francisco had the misfortune of being located at the epicenter of the quake that destroyed the city. In the aftermath, a fire broke out which reduced every building to a pile of ashes.

Mr. Kerr, with the rest of the residents of that part of the city were evacuated and not permitted to enter for several days. Mr. Kerr's friends came to him and expressed their sympathy for the loss of his factory. They knew that this disaster had financially wiped him out. However, Mr. Kerr was a tithe-paying Christian and believed that God would keep His Word and rebuke the devourer for his sake.

When the officials finally gave permission for the land owners to return to their destroyed homes and property, Mr. Kerr slowly walked through the charred streets of burnt ruble in the direction of his factory. Nothing survived the catastrophe, but in the distance, he saw the wooden fence which surrounded his property. He came to the gate and discovered that the fire had come right up to the wooden fence, singed some paint, and then mysteriously stopped.

The building that housed his glass factory was still standing and when he opened the door, to his amazement, not one glass, fruit jar, or anything else had been jolted from the shelf. His factory was still intact and unharmed even though it was in the epicenter of one of the 20th century's worst disasters. Through Mr. Kerr's commitment to Jesus, faith in His promises, and obedience to His Word, he had created a spiritual and financial Goshen. Neither fire nor earthquake could cross the border into his Goshen.

Perhaps you find yourself at the epicenter of the worst disaster of your life. Perhaps there is an intuitive fear that the worst is still to come, but there is a place you can go where the plagues cannot follow. Run to Jesus and let him protect and preserve you in the land of Goshen.

On October 16, 1991, at Luby's Cafeteria in Kileen, Texas, a deranged man drove his pickup through the plate glass window. He got out of his pickup truck with a Glock 17 pistol and Ruger P89 revolver. He took careful aim at the patrons of this restaurant, and within minutes 23 people lay dead and another 20 wounded. In the midst of this shooting spree, the gunmen fired on the people in the cafeteria line. Only one person in the line survived, an African American lady who often dined there. Everyone in front of her and behind her was killed. She left this scene of mass murder unscathed.

When reporters asked for the reason that she was spared while everyone else was shot, she explained what happened. She told the reporters that the gunmen aimed his pistol right at her. She made eye contact with this mad man and said to him, "the blood of Jesus is against you." Something supernatural happened next. It was as if an invisible hand pushed the gun away. Faith in the power of the blood shielded this woman from certain destruction. A madman on a killing rampage could not cross the border into her spiritual Goshen.

## IN 1985, A COLUMBIAN MOUNTAIN CALLED NEVADO DEL RUIZ BEGAN TO RUMBLE AND SPEW STEAM AND ASH.

There were several cities on the mountain side and nearby valley who were told by their government that they were in no immediate danger. However, one September night when most of the residents were asleep, magma spewed out of the volcano and traveled down the mountain at 450 miles per hour. The magma flow totally destroyed the cities of Chinchina and Armero. Twenty two thousand people were buried under tons of hot mud and another 10,000 were left homeless. When the rescuers reached Armero, they were shocked by the devastation and shocked even more by a few people they found in a small Full Gospel church.

**26**

The church was standing among flattened buildings. The flow of mud mixed with magma split when it approached the church, streamed on both sides of the building, and then came together on the other side to continued its path of destruction. The small gathering of believers who were safe inside, all had the same story. They were asleep and awakened by the Holy Spirit and told to run quickly to the church. It was almost midnight when they arrived. They entered the doors of God's House just before the mountain exploded and rivers of mud came crashing down upon their city.

Psalm 46:1-3 (King James Version)

*God is our refuge and strength, a very present help in trouble.*

*Therefore will not we fear, though the earth be removed, and though the mountains be carried into the midst of the sea;*

*Though the waters thereof roar and be troubled, though the mountains shake with the swelling thereof. Selah.*

They didn't know that God's intervening power literally made their little church an island of safety in a sea of destruction. These Spirit-filled believers were dwelling in Goshen and the flow of hot magma from an erupting volcano could not cross the border.

It is time to move our spiritual address to Goshen, leave the Egypt of unbelief, come out of a sin-cursed world, flee the dry desert of religious formalism, and discover the favor of the Lord in a place that is overshadowed with His wings. Life is good in Goshen!

# CHAPTER 2

# TAKE UP THY BED
## (ROLLING UP THE YESTERDAYS)

*Mark 2:11 I say unto thee, Arise, and take up thy bed, and go thy way into thine house.*

*And immediately he arose, took up the bed, and went forth before them all; insomuch that they were all amazed, and glorified God, saying, We never saw it on this fashion.*

The atmosphere of Goshen can become the reality of any believer who diligently obeys the Lord's instructions. It is possible through the power of the Holy Spirit to be exempt from the curses and wretchedness that blight our times. (I John 5:18)

The believer who is surrounded with the atmosphere of Goshen can be the exception to the normal course of things. Healing exempts from disease. Faith exempts from despair. The joy of the Lord exempts from the sorrow of this present age.

The Spirit of God is ready to duplicate the plague-stopping conditions of Goshen for His Endtime covenant people. The blessings enumerated in His Word are intended to overtake us in these chaotic days and transform us into mighty overcomers.

It is worth probing the Word of God to discover those principles and truths which bring us into the exceptional reality of divine preservation. The miracles of Jesus do more than document the release of His supernatural power. The manifestations of His Spirit reveal the things that we can expect in spiritual Goshen. It is in these displays of His glory that we learn to apply the truth that sets the captive free.

The central message in His miracles instruct the believer in the practical aspects of transforming our surroundings to an area where curses cannot operate. Our goal should be to dwell so close to the Presence of the Lord that plagues are unable to reach us. (Ps. 91:1)

The healing of the paralytic demonstrates the first principle of establishing a Goshen-like environment. No one can move forward to better things who is unwilling to roll up the failures and hurts of yesterday. The pain, bitterness, disappointment, and heartache of the past can paralyze our spirit and prevent us from entering into our inheritance.

Unforgiveness can become a literal death-bed to ministry, happiness, and longevity of life. Old habits, addictions, and worldly attachments, which so many are reluctant to surrender to God, will force a person to lie down on a cot of misery and wasted efforts.

If we are to recover from all the things which paralyze our progress, then the spiritual and mental "bed-roll" must be taken up and permanently put away. Every believer has been tackled by reversals and unexpected setbacks, but instead of listening to those voices that are trying to keep us immobilized, we need to hear a fresh word from the Lord. The timeless words of Jesus to every believer yearning to move forward is "arise, take up thy bed and walk."

We must constantly remember that the words of our Master are far greater than the theories and conjectures of men. Man is unable to arrive at absolute facts because he doesn't possess total information and data on anything. He doesn't know all there is to know about the universe, the environment, the atmosphere, or even his own anatomy.

Observation alone can never reveal the whole story. Facts keep changing as more knowledge is accumulated. Much of what is called "science" today was called "science fiction" yesterday. And the assumed facts which are believed to govern nature now may have to be revised as man is ever learning but never able to come to the knowledge of the truth.

However, the Word of God never needs to be revised or updated. It is the ultimate source of knowledge. It is Truth which never changes. The immutable and unchanging God imparted Himself into His Word so His creative and redemptive power could continually be manifested in the Earth. We know Him through His Word.

*2 Tim 3:16-17 (King James Version)*

*All scripture is given by inspiration of God, and is profitable for doctrine, for reproof, for correction, for instruction in righteousness:*

*That the man of God may be perfect, thoroughly furnished unto all good works.*

The written Word of God is more than sacred literature. It is a life-giving message that must be heralded with divine authority. Everything changes when the Word of God is spoken into it. Speak the Word into the atmosphere and the enemy must vacate the immediate surroundings. Speak the Word into the human heart and a person's nature changes from destructive darkness into marvelous light. Speak the Word into drastic difficulties and the demonic underpinnings of trouble collapse.

There is a life force in the Word of God that can't be denied. Jesus healed, cast out devils, raised the dead, and stilled the storm with His Word.

**The words and works of men will fade away, but the Word of the Lord is forever.**

God's immutable Word spans the generations. It is relevant to every age. It is above time and the intellectually fashionable ideologies of our day. The philosophies of men change as quickly as clothing styles. Communism was once fashionable among developing nations, but no more. Fascism at one time was considered to be the wave of the future, but hardly anyone today can define it.

According to the Scriptures; atheism, agnosticism, humanism, socialism, hedonism, and all the other godless "isms" of men are headed for the ash heap of history. But the Word of the Lord will remain forever. *"Heaven and earth shall pass away, but my words shall not pass away."* (Matt. 24:35 King James Version)

**It is because the Word of God is everlasting that we can trust it without reservation.**

After we place our trust in the Word of God, then it is absolutely necessary to develop a mind that can comprehend and apply its divine truth.

*1 Corinthians 2:14 (King James Version)*

*But the natural man receiveth not the things of the Spirit of God: for they are foolishness unto him: neither can he know them, because they are spiritually discerned.*

The Apostle Paul made a distinction between those who are held captive by the limitations of the lower nature and those who function with a mind that has been renewed by the Spirit of God.

A person in a carnal, unsaved, unregenerate state cannot receive the things of the Spirit. The glory, wonder, liberty and truth of the Kingdom seem foolish to the person whose mind is dominated by the darkness of a sinful culture. The laws which govern the Kingdom of God are completely illogical to a person with a secular world view. The fleshly mind cannot associate giving with increase, sacrifice with abundance, or submission with freedom. They can't understand the difference between religion and relationship.

However, the person with a renewed mind and a changed heart lives in an enlightened state of reality where the end of a matter is understood from the beginning. *"And we know that all things work together for good to them that love God, to them who are the called according to his purpose." (Romans 8:28 King James Version)*

A renewed mind, changed by the Spirit of God, is essential in understanding the promises and prerogatives of the born-again believer. In this critical hour, the believer needs something more than mere information about the miraculous power of God. We need divine intervention in every level of our existence. Intervention in the lives of God's redeemed is the precise reason that the Holy Spirit was sent to indwell us.

Intervention with the goal of transforming the believer into the image of Christ is the specific task of the Holy Spirit today. He reproves, guides, comforts, teaches and leads. The final passage in Mark's Gospel is a testimony to the intervening work of the Holy Spirit: *"And they went forth, and preached everywhere, the Lord working with them, and confirming the word with signs following." (Mark 16:20 King James Version)*

The "signs" were substantiating miracles verifying the authority of the Word. The confirmation of the preached Word of God is still the mission of the Holy Spirit. The Greek word translated "confirm" in our English Bibles actually means "to establish, to make steadfast, to stabilize". Faith in the mighty promises moves the Holy Spirit to establish

**33**

a spiritual Goshen around the believer to preserve and protect us in perilous times.

Only those with a spiritual mind can receive instruction on how to live in a Goshen-like state until Jesus calls
us home.

> *1 Corinthians 2:12-13 (King James Version)*
>
> *Now we have received, not the spirit of the world,
> but the spirit which is of God; that we might know
> the things that are freely given to us of God.*
>
> *Which things also we speak, not in the words
> which man's wisdom teacheth, but which the Holy
> Ghost teacheth; comparing spiritual things with
> spiritual.*

**All believers will be greatly changed when they
receive the revelation of the five things which Jesus
said to take up.**

There are five things which Jesus specifically commanded to be taken up. These five things illustrate the
truths which transform our reality into a spiritual Goshen.

The four Gospels record only five instances where
Jesus commanded His followers to take up something that
released their breakthrough. The Spirit of God placed these
five commands in the Word to do more than merely benefit
those who heard it first. These commands are relevant to
believers who are living in the Endtime.

Notice, first of all, that five is the number of grace.
There were five offerings in the Old Testament system
for approaching God: the **burnt** offering, **peace** offering,
**sin** offering, **trespass** offering, and **meat** offering. There
are five ministries in the New Testament era: apostles,
prophets, evangelists, pastors, and teachers. The number "five" is mentioned 318 times in the Bible and always

refers to the goodness and grace of God (underserved favor).

There are five women in the genealogy of the Lord: Rahab, Ruth, Tamar, Bathsheba, and Mary. With the exception of Mary, the other four women were nefarious individuals. Bathsheba committed adultery with David. Tamar was a prostitute. Ruth was a hated Moabite. Rahab was a harlot. These women are found in the genealogy of Jesus because God wanted us to understand Messiah doesn't come through Law, but through Grace.

When we read in the Gospels about five things which Jesus said to take up, we are reading about the goodness and unmerited favor of God.

The phrase "take up" requires some explanation. It is really just one Greek word with a variety of meanings. It "means to lift up from the ground, to move from its place, to take by force, or to cause to cease." The Greek word for take up is a word that demands a specific response from those to whom it is spoken. The Lord did not issue this command so that it would be analyzed. He intended for us to obey it.

When Jesus said "take up", He was demanding that something specific be done. Their was no time to analyze. Immediate response was required. It was an emphatic command demanding instant action. Failure to immediately obey meant the loss of a miracle.

The people who heard Him say those two mighty words understood they could not delay.

Any student of Bible prophecy realizes that there have been many delays in the fulfillment of God's prophetic plan. However, there is a moment coming when a heavenly messenger will announce "no more delays". Often believers feel that God's promise for their personal deliverance has been postponed, but the latest movements in the spirit realm suggest that we are in a time of acceleration. The message of this moment is NO MORE DELAYS.

Revelation 10:5-7 (King James Version)

*And the angel which I saw stand upon the sea and upon the earth lifted up his hand to heaven,*

*And sware by him that liveth for ever and ever, who created heaven, and the things that therein are, and the earth, and the things that therein are, and the sea, and the things which are therein, that there should be time no longer: (no more delays)*

*But in the days of the voice of the seventh angel, when he shall begin to sound, the mystery of God should be finished, as he hath declared to his servants the prophets.*

It is not my intention to take this Scripture out of its prophetic context. Bible students understand that the event in this passage transpires during the mid-way point of the seven years of Tribulation. However, this future occurrence reveals something about God's operation in every block of time. There is a spiritual truth in this prophetic event which is applicable to us today.

Notice that the gesture of this heavenly messenger accelerated God's prophetic plan. The Angel of the Lord lifted up his hand to end the hindrances and setbacks. He put one foot on the land and another on the sea, and once this stand was taken, he lifted his hand to intensify the workings of God in the earth. The raising of his hand to Heaven triggered greater things. Every time Jesus told somebody to take something up, it meant that His plan had reached critical mass.

Small anointed gestures produce great miracles. Anointing with oil is a small gesture, but it brings powerful deliverances and mighty healings. Praise is dismissed as just noise made by radical believers in a heightened state of emotional excitement, but it is more than a meaningless gesture or hollow shout. Praise actually triggers the miraculous. Lifting up our hands and our voice quickens God's time table. We can speed up the process of divine intervention through praise.

It is not only strange, but hypocritical, if not blasphemous, for emotion and excitement to be socially acceptable in every kind of gathering except in the House of God. Political rallies would be counterproductive if the supporters were silent and motionless. Professional sports would soon cease if the fans sat mute in the stands. Celebrities would be quickly forgotten and the film industry bankrupt if cheering crowds were replaced by soundless bystanders.

The noise of cheering followers and supporters is not just accepted, but expected at most secular gatherings, but this same culture denigrates any expression and gesture of praise to our Savior and Lord. If the church is to duplicate the conditions of Goshen and draw near to His Presence, then the role of praise to our existence must be understood.

We cannot tolerate dead, dry, and lifeless funeral-like services. The Psalmist was aware of unhealthy trends that would attempt to silence praise under the guise of refinement and dignity. He penetrated the veneer of pride by contrasting the praisers with the non-praisers. His words are poignant and explicit:

*Psalm 115:17 (King James Version)*

*The dead praise not the LORD, neither any that go down into silence.*

*But we will bless the LORD from this time forth and for evermore. Praise the LORD.*

When the believers arrive at God's House, we ought to be praising Him with one voice. No one should have to be cajoled or coaxed into Spirit anointed worship. Even without a choir or a song, we are to "enter into his gates with thanksgiving, and into his courts with praise: . . ." (Ps. 110:4 King James Version)

Such glorious praise in the House of God will bring His Glory. The Glory of the Lord has the potential of releasing the awesome power of resurrection. Jesus raised His face to the Father in prayer and then commanded Lazarus to come out of the tomb. The original words in His command convey the concept of force. The words which brought Lazarus from the tomb refer to the impartation of strength to perform something that was formerly impossible. Dwelling in spiritual Goshen means that God is working to empower His people to do those things which could not be done before.

The command to "take up" means that power is immediately available to get things off the ground. So many believers are having trouble getting their marriage, business, or dream off the ground. There is a point in the Presence of the Lord when He says "take up." On the strength of His command, we are then able to perform mighty exploits, achieve great victories, and experience miraculous accomplishments.

If faith is combined with sensitivity to the Spirit, the empty hands of those who read this book will soon be filled with power. The "take up anointing" is presently spreading through the Body of Christ with amazing speed.

### In Matthew 9:6, the paralytic is told to take up his bed and walk.

Three of the Gospel narratives include the miracle of the man who was carried on his bed and lowered through a roof, so that he could be healed. There was an obstacle to this man's healing. Any time God ordains someone to be delivered, the enemy will resist and hinder. Healing never happens without a battle. Breakthroughs only occur when the obstruction is overcome. These four men had enough compassion on their paralyzed friend, and determination to overcome any hindrance, to get him to Jesus.

**While they pursued their goal, they discovered that something had to be torn up before this man could get into the Presence of the Lord**.

A crowd kept these four buddies from getting their hopeless friend to the Master. The people in attendance displayed a selfish attitude and cynical spirit. None of them had enough sympathy to give their place to a man who desperately needed the touch of the Master's hand. Luke tells us that the house was filled with Pharisees and doctors of the law. They all just stubbornly kept their place. They had no regard for the suffering of this poor paralytic who couldn't walk, or stand, or move.

It is ironic that this crowd knew the Scriptures, but couldn't understand the Word. They were steeped in their tradition and had come to find fault. These critics wouldn't step aside to let a sick man experience healing. Even though the atmosphere of the house was poisoned with animosity and judgmentalism, nothing could stop the Lord from being who He was. In spite of all the negative influences in the atmosphere, there was a Healer in the house.

The Pharisees and doctors of the Law sat with a smug look on their face. They were intent on inventing some new accusation against the Master. They were adept at twisting the statements of their opponents against them. Jesus was their target that day, but none of their evil intentions prevailed.

Critics couldn't stop Him then, and they can't stop Him now. He never placated their concerns. He never once hesitated to meet the urgent needs of suffering humanity out of fear that it might offend someone's theological sensibilities.

The record of the Scripture is that the power of the Lord was present to heal, but the man who needed the healing was outside, unable to enter because of all that unbelief.

It was evident to the four that something had to be torn up. The four determined men tore up the roof to lower their paralyzed friend into the presence of Jesus. The structure wasn't as important as making contact with the Great Physician.

There is a growing realization among today's believers that personal agendas, organizational structures, denominational proclivities, and traditional procedures may have to be torn up to get the hurting into the Presence of the Lord. Preconceived notions based on a person's personal preferences instead of the Word of God must be dismantled because the needs are so urgent.

These four determined men refused to miss their moment out of some superficial consideration for something as temporary as a roof. They were actually removing the arbitrary limits from faith. The Lord viewed the demolition of the roof as faith in action. Faith still tears up the hindrances that obstruct the way into the Presence of the Lord.

Those four men did more than destroy a roof; they demolished the atmosphere of unbelief inside the house. The disturbance broke the stagnant mood of the crowd. All the Pharisees were knocked off balance. Anticipation inflamed the people as the same question entered everyone's mind: what is Jesus going to do now?

Expectation activated faith for healing. Perhaps the greatest need in the Body of Christ is for another spiritual demolition crew to arrive on the scene. It should be noted that they didn't touch the foundation of the house. The foundation wasn't the problem, the roof was the hindrance. The structure had to be altered to provide an entrance for a suffering man to reach the Master.

It is all too common in our time for so-called movers and shakers of the American church to deliberately tamper with the foundation in an effort to accommodate the culture. There is an appalling and alarming trend away from the Scriptures as the infallible Word of God, from a personal experience of salvation, from prayer as the believer's power source, and from the anointing of the Holy Spirit as the means to overcome. These are the foundations of a real relationship with God, but they are being undermined by the popularity of new approaches.

The Apostle Paul stressed that Jesus is the irreplaceable foundation. (I Cor. 3:11) He warned that everyone must be careful of the materials we select to build on the foundation. (I Cor. 3:10) It should be acknowledged that wood, hay, and stubble will not endure and will be eventually consumed. The superficial should be exchanged for the supernatural. It would be awesome if God's people wondered once more, "What is Jesus going to do now?"

I am not suggesting spiritual anarchy, because the Scriptural admonition is that "everything be done decently and in order." However, it should be understood that there is a difference between order and form.

The Holy Spirit has divine order to all of His workings, but we often hinder His operation with our forms and traditions. The roof in the house served a practical purpose until Jesus entered. The roof seemed to be a necessary part of the structure, but the Lord had never been in that house before.

The house became too small for the Presence of the Lord. The structure was too confining for the power that was active that day. The roof became an obstacle and a hindrance. It had to come off to make way for a miracle.

Nothing in the Scripture happened by accident. The Spirit of God orchestrated the events of that day to illustrate a timeless lesson for those who are serious about pursuing His Presence. The four men who tore up the roof were not acting in a disorderly manner. They were removing the limitations, the barriers, and the hindrances which blocked the way to miracles.

Tradition, format, ritual and theological constraints can block our way to the Presence, just as surely as the roof hindered the paralyzed man from receiving healing. However, those who are driven by a consuming desire to bring impossible situations before the Lord will not stand on ceremony or protocol. They will find a way into the Presence of Jesus.

The cries for revival that preceded the great awakenings in our nation's past are seldom heard anymore. Yet there is a remnant which yearns for the reality of God's mighty power. Though few in number, faithful believers can still be heard to pray, "revive thy works in the midst of the years."

Recently, there has appeared some indication that the surviving church is on the verge of receiving its answer to our pleas for a fresh outpouring of His Spirit. However a word of caution is needed. Revivals are messy affairs. The status quo will be interrupted. Church as usual will be no more because the Holy Spirit will force people from their comfort zones. When the Lord enters the House, the roof will come off.

**There is a stark choice looming before us: either preserve the structure or pursue the Presence.**

When the roof comes off, the bed rolls of yesterday will be vacated and taken up. No one who came to the house in Capernaum that day expected the ceiling to be broken up and a paralyzed man to take up his bed and walk. But where the power of the Lord is present to heal, the unexpected always happens.

The mat upon which the sick man laid was designed for the hopeless. It was where people with no answer laid in embarrassment and want. The only world the paralytic knew was his bed.

The sick were laid on these "mats" so they could be transported from place to place. Their only hope of livelihood was begging. Some kind people would put them in crowded places and leave them to beg for leftovers. When people are paralyzed, leftovers are all they can expect. Whether the paralysis is physical, mental, financial or spiritual, the helpless are dependent on leftovers. People who lay in their misery, bitterness, and disappointment are compelled to exist on scraps. They experience only little snippets of joy and happiness. Their pre-occupation with the past soon eclipses all hope for the future.

Just one encounter with the Master is enough to roll up all of our yesterdays. Believers who are stuck in difficulties and trapped in despair can know the incredible liberty that comes when He says, "Take up thy bed and walk".

Four men told the man they couldn't raise him from the bed, but they could carry him to someone who delivers. It is my prayer that God will raise up the same caliber of compassionate believer today. Not a lot of people will answer the call. But there are still a capable few who can take both the person and the problem to the Master.

There is a unique reward in bringing the paralyzed to the feet of Jesus. The joy on the rooftop must have been uncontainable as the four witnessed the Lord heal their hopeless friend. He laid in impossibility for a long time. His situation deteriorated with every passing day. The paralysis was spreading. His body was weakening. Time was running out.

Jesus first dealt with his most urgent need. The sin in his soul was more serious than the paralysis in his body. The Master always goes to the heart of the matter. The Lord never deals with symptoms and neglects the source. Healing went first to the paralytic's soul before it reached his emaciated body.

The first words Jesus spoke to this bed-ridden sufferer were "son, thy sins be forgiven thee." The Lord brought the hidden condition of this man to the surface. He could not fulfill his dreams as long as his sin kept him paralyzed. Sin had undermined his destiny and immobilized him. If he were to ever walk again, then sin's hold had to be broken.

The connection between sin and sickness is still an issue which few believers fully understand. The Scriptures reveal that disease is an oppression of the devil (Acts 10:38,

Luke 13:16) Affliction is a weapon used by our archenemy to "steal, kill, and destroy."

The Scriptures also reveal that overt sin is an invitation for disease to enter.

Psalm 107:17 (King James Version)

*"Fools because of their transgression, and because of their iniquities, are afflicted. Their soul abhorreth all manner of meat; and they draw near unto the gates of death.*

Sin is the breeding ground for sickness. Our archenemy is the purveyor of death and looks for opportunities to bring a premature end to every life. Sin provides him an entrance.

However, not every victim of disease is afflicted because of some personal sin. The disciples made the mistake of thinking that all sickness was punishment for individual sin. (John 9:2) The Lord corrected their erroneous theology and revealed that He had come to manifest the works of God against disease. Sickness and illness plague the human race because of Adam's fall, but the power of Jesus' shed blood can reverse the curse.

Jesus is the answer for the source, symptom, cause and effect of disease. It was to silence all questions about His authority to forgive sin that He said to the sick of the palsy, "arise, take up thy bed, and go thy way into thine house."

The Lord always instructs people to do something with their paralyzing situation. Whatever constitutes the bed upon which the victim is laying must be taken up in victory.

The mat of the paralytic was thought to be his deathbed by the culture of the times. These mats often became the casket bearing the diseased and infirm to the grave.

However, instead of being carried to the grave, this man was carried to Jesus. His encounter with the Lord changed everything.

Once the bed held him, but after receiving a word from the Lord, the man went away holding the bed. The fears, the dreaded diagnosis, the dismal future, the failures of yesterday, and the disappointments were rolled up in that mat and carried away.

It sounds simplistic to a culture which blames every deplorable condition on the injustice and hurt of our former years, that an encounter with Jesus will roll up the past. But it is true. The effects of drugs, alcohol, rejection, abuse, and hurts so deep that neither therapy nor personality-altering medication can reach it, can be rolled up and carried away.

A rolled up past brought the release which prompted the Apostle Paul to write, "forgetting those things which are behind, and reaching forth unto those things which are before, I press toward the mark for the prize of the high calling of God in Christ Jesus." (Phillipians 3:13)

It was iron in his soul that enabled Joseph to roll up his past and brought him out of the pit to the palace. He celebrated his deliverance from the past by calling his firstborn "Manasseh" which means "God hath made me forget".

It was Job's intercessory prayer that rolled up the sorrow of his yesterdays, turned his captivity, and brought more blessings in his latter years than in his beginning. (Job. 42:12)

**Jesus will turn the situation around for those who take up their bed.**

The Scripture said that the occupants of the house were all amazed and glorified God when paralyzed limbs moved in response to a word from the Lord. The sight of a terminally ill patient rising from his death bed was overwhelming. No one

**45**

thought about the demolished roof. No one considered the theological viewpoints of the Pharisees. The unbelief and cynicism that had earlier dominated the atmosphere was gone. The paralytic was paralyzed no more. He paraded up and down the house with his rolled up mat. As he left the building, the amazed people said, "We never saw it on this fashion."

Unprecedented things happen when people take up their bed and walk. The mundane, ordinary, and routine way of living is no more. The blocks and hindrances to greater glory are gone. Unexciting church services are replaced with times of refreshing from the Presence of the Lord. The common is replaced with an uncommon anointing of the Holy Spirit. The mighty manifestations of God's miraculous power will have people saying again, "we never saw it on this fashion."

**The borders of a spiritual Goshen are established by believers who refuse to be shackled by yesterday**.

Dr. Kenneth Wuest, a New Testament Greek scholar, accurately translated the Lord's instruction to the paralytic. From the original language of the New Testament, Dr. Wuest translated the words of Jesus to say "Be arising and start walking, and keep on walking."

Borders are established by the footprints of the redeemed. The Lord said to Abraham, "Arise, walk through the land in the length of it and in the breadth of it: for I will give it thee." (Gen. 13:17)

The command to establish borders was handed down to all the descendants of Abraham.

*Every place whereon the soles of your feet shall tread shall be yours:* . . . Deuteronomy 11:24

The mandate to set up a perimeter of faith which stops the plague is now our promise and perogative.

However, no one can establish borders with paralyzed feet. Once we have rolled up the attitudes, conditions, heartbreaks, and lingering bitterness of the past, our feet are free to establish a spiritual Goshen in a darkened world.

The word of the Lord is not isolated to just one paralytic. His command for all is "Be arising and start walking, and keep on walking." Walk by faith and establish the borders of your personal Goshen.

# CHAPTER 3

# TAKE UP THE CROSS
## (ENTRY LEVEL CHRISTIANITY)

Luke 9:23

*"And he said to them all, If any man will come after me, let him deny himself, and take up his cross daily, and follow me."*

Creating a modern day Goshen in our experience requires something that the old Adamic nature will resist. The tendencies toward evil in the human soul must be dealt with in a manner that ensures it will not dominate or dictate our behavior. The blessings of divine prosperity and preservation depend on submitting to the control of the Holy Spirit. The desires of the carnal nature is an enemy to the Spirit of God. A love and attachment to the world is evidence that a person has been capitivated by the spirit of Egypt. The word that is used in the Scripture to describe the appetites and indulges for wrong doing is "flesh".

Jesus said, "The flesh profiteth nothing." (John 6:63 King James Version)

The Apostle Paul warned of yielding to ungodly inner desires:

Romans 7:5 (King James Version)

*For when we were in the flesh, the motions of sins, which were by the law, did work in our members to bring forth fruit unto death.*

Most of the book of Romans is devoted to the dangers of permitting the old nature to rule our thoughts and conduct. With raw candor the Word of God bluntly states the eternal consequences of permitting the flesh to govern.

Romans 8:13 (King James Version)

*For if ye live after the flesh, ye shall die: but if ye through the Spirit do mortify the deeds of the body, ye shall live.*

The Galatian believers had been seduced by Jewish adherents into the bondage of Mosaic Law. They were deceived into believing that the rituals and ceremonies of Judaism could substitute for a self-desciplined life which brings true liberty in Christ. The Law was powerless to prevent the flesh from taking over. So the Apostle Paul revealed the only way of dealing with it.

Gal 5:24 (King James Version)

*And they that are Christ's have crucified the flesh with the affections and lusts.*

Crucifying the flesh is Paul's terminology for an experience that sets the believer apart from immorality and corruption. In his personal testimony to the Galatians, the Apostle revealed that a life of victory and liberty is possible through the Spirit of God.

*Gal 2:20*

*I am crucified with Christ: nevertheless I live; yet not I, but Christ liveth in me: and the life which I now live in the flesh I live by the faith of the Son of God, who loved me, and gave himself for me.*

The Apostle's writing elaborates on the Lord's command to take up the Cross. The old nature must be nailed to the Cross. The Cross must be in our preaching, our singing, our teaching, and our lifestyle. The message of the Cross is indispensable. It entails more than the price the Redeemer paid for our salvation. It speaks of the believer's obligation to renounce the old life with its "affections and lusts." (Gal. 5:24)

There is no way of getting around the Master's command. He was explicit in his directive. Following Jesus means daily taking up the Cross.

A common misconception has endured through the years that hardships, handicaps, and chronic misery constitute our cross. But most adversity is either the result of satanic attack or reaping for unrepented sins.

The real cross of the believer is personal and practical. It means to set the will of God above our own desires and ambitions. It means a life void of lust and sinful yearnings. It means commitment and obedience to the Word of God. It means to serve Him with all our heart. It means to be spiritual instead of carnal. It means a life controlled by the Spirit instead of ruled by the flesh.

**Taking up the cross puts us in conflict with the culture and religious trends**.

Our humanistic society has infiltrated the church and is attempting to rid the Christian faith of the Cross. The Cross is directly opposed to everything that the world advocates. The culture insists that there are no absolutes. According to

**51**

modern thought, everything is relative. However, the Cross represents absolute truth revealed in the Word of God. It is the only anchor in a world that is falling apart.

Our culture postulates that there is no answer for the human condition. The popular consensus is that man is forever enslaved to his inner passions and desires. They contend that nothing more can be done other than simply to suppress lustful appetites or accept the problem as normal. Addictions abound and the only treatment available are questionable therapies with little results.

The Cross, however, stands like a beacon in the darkness to show the way of escape from the bondages, addictions, and guilt of the fallen nature. The culture's method of dealing with sin is to deny its existance. The existence of sin in the human heart is a concept scoffed at by society's movers and shakers. Yet, the Cross not only testifies to sin's awful reality, it provides the only remedy for man's depraved condition.

The culture enshrines the flesh, but the Cross crucifies it.

The culture has raised selfishness to a virtue, but the Cross destroys all egocentric tendencies.

The culture is dominated by demonic powers, but the Cross defeats sin, the flesh, and the devil. The Cross is a "no trespassing sign" to principalities and powers, denying them any access to the soul.

When the culture is examined, it is plain to see that it offers no hope for the future, but the Cross is the bridge to a bright tomorrow in the City where the Lamb is the light.

The culture has paved the broadway of destruction with licentiousness, perversion, and immorality. The Cross provides a turn around so that the repentant soul can change directions.

Sin is the problem, the Cross is the answer.

Salvation begins with a choice between the culture and the Cross. It has always been so. There will never be a time when the true meaning of "taking up the cross" will be accepted by a pleasure crazed world. The Cross is unattractive to those who spend every waking moment satisfying carnal cravings.

The attack on the Cross springs from an attempt to make Christianity more acceptable to the unsaved. The Cross carries a reproach. It marks a person as separate from the crowd. It offends a lost world. Even in the earliest times of Christianity, the Cross was attacked.

Gal. 5:11 (New International Version)

*"Brothers, if I am still preaching circumcision, why am I still being persecuted. In that case the offense of the cross has been abolished."*

The word "offense" is actually "skandalon" in the original Greek language. We get our word scandal from it. It is a reference to the criticisms and opinions of people who reproach the believer for taking a stand against sin and refusing to participate in the lifestyles of the wicked.

The offense of the Cross is the abuse directed against real Christians for having convictions and placing our relationship with Jesus above everything else. Our commitment to the Lord is above patriotism, citizenship, political loyalties, friendships, and career. Nothing can be permitted to sever our connection with God. The offense of the Cross entails a litany of pejoratives and derogatory names directed against the believer. Without hesitation, the enemies of the Gospel will call us fanatics, radicals, homophobes, and many other shameful names. Almost every day the world invents a new accusation, a new smear, and a new label to deprecate God's people. However, their hateful treatment of the redeemed has no effect. We have nailed these offenses to the Cross.

It must be remembered that persecution always backfires.

**53**

1 Peter 4:14 (King James Version)

*If ye be reproached for the name of Christ, happy are ye; for the spirit of glory and of God resteth upon you: on their part he is evil spoken of, but on your part he is glorified.*

Many have portrayed the Cross as legalism and asceticism. It is neither. Taking up the cross means total surrender and complete dedication to the Master. The Cross is freedom from the flesh nature. It is the power to live godly.

Those who take up the cross understand Paul's elation.

Gal 6:14 (King James Version)

*But God forbid that I should glory, save in the cross of our Lord Jesus Christ, by whom the world is crucified unto me, and I unto the world.*

The reason the enemy never tires in his plots to remove the Cross from our experience is because he is totally disarmed by it. Every demonic philosophy is overthrown by the Cross. Every satanic weapon is rendered useless by the Cross.

1 Corinthians 1:19-21 (King James Version)

*For it is written, I will destroy the wisdom of the wise, and will bring to nothing the understanding of the prudent. Where is the wise? where is the scribe? where is the disputer of this world? hath not God made foolish the wisdom of this world?*

*For after that in the wisdom of God the world by wisdom knew not God, it pleased God by the foolishness of preaching to save them that believe.*

54

1 Corinthians 1:18 (King James Version)

*For the preaching of the cross is to them that perish foolishness; but unto us which are saved it is the power of God.*

The true Gospel extols the triumphs of the Cross.

Five times in the Gospels, Jesus commanded His disciples to take up the Cross and follow Him. He put some tough requirements on being His disciple.

Matt 10:38 (King James Version)

*And he that taketh not his cross, and followeth after me, is not worthy of me.*

Luke 14:27 (King James Version)

*And whosoever doth not bear his cross, and come after me, cannot be my disciple.*

The rich young ruler came to Jesus with an urgent question. He felt the need in his soul for salvation. He was moral, upright, and devout, but there was something missing. He questioned the Lord, "what must I do to inherit eternal life?"

The Lord quoted the commandments to him. The young aristocrat replied that he kept all the commandments from his childhood, yet there was something lacking. Jesus said to him, "sell whatsoever thou hast, and give to the poor, and thou shalt have treasure in heaven: and come, take up the cross, and follow me."

The young man had the character, the desire, and the will to please God. He had a longing to be holy. He wanted to be righteous. However, he couldn't handle the Cross. The Cross meant dying out to the things that he loved, and he loved his possessions. The Cross was the only way that this man could obtain the giving spirit which is a necessary part of following Jesus.

In the end, he forfeited eternal life in favor of goods that he could not keep. Sadly, multitudes are making the same mistake today.

1 Timothy 6:17 (King James Version)

*Charge them that are rich in this world, that they be not highminded, nor trust in uncertain riches, but in the living God, who giveth us richly all things to enjoy;*

We cannot follow Him without a cross. Without commitment, there will be no reward. Without surrender, there will be no victory. Without dedication, there will be no deliverance. Without brokenness, there will be no blessing. Without giving, there will be no receiving. Without faith, there will be no answer. Without a personal encounter with the Cross, there will be no triumphant resurrection.

**The Cross is more than self denial, it cancels the curse.**

The Persians, Phoenicians, Greeks, and Romans executed their victims on a cross, but the Jewish method of execution was stoning. Only after the person was killed did their dead bodies hang on a cross or a tree to show that they died as the cursed of God. The Law of Moses said the corpse of criminals and law-breakers were to hang on a tree. Joshua hung the five bodies of Canaanite kings on a tree to demonstrate that their enemies were cursed. The Gibeonites hung seven men in retaliation for Saul's atrocities because their involvement unleashed a curse.

Jesus had to die on a cross to cancel the curses that sin brought on the human race.

Gal 3:13-14 (King James Version)

*Christ hath redeemed us from the curse of the law, being made a curse for us: for it is written, Cursed is every one that hangeth on a tree: That the blessing of Abraham might come on the Gentiles through Jesus Christ; that we might receive the promise of the Spirit through faith.*

The Cross should be regarded as a symbol of power, not just death. The blood upon the cross is the only source of peace from God. It alone has the power to replace the curse with blessings.

Col 1:20-22 (King James Version)

*And, having made peace through the blood of his cross, by him to reconcile all things unto himself; by him, I say, whether they be things in earth, or things in heaven.*

*And you, that were sometime alienated and enemies in your mind by wicked works, yet now hath he reconciled in the body of his flesh through death, to present you holy and unblameable and unreproveable in his sight."*

**The Cross is where the writ of execution was posted.**

No one was hung on a cross without a document that told the crimes for which the guilty man was executed. A sign would be placed around the felon's neck listing the crimes he committed and read by those attending his execution. They would then nail the sign to the top of the cross. In the case of Jesus, His writ of execution was written in three languages which simply stated, "This is Jesus of Nazareth, the King of the Jews." But the Apostle Paul received a revelation that more than just Pilate's words were nailed to the Cross of Jesus.

**57**

Col 2:14 (King James Version)

*Blotting out the handwriting of ordinances that was against us, which was contrary to us, and took it out of the way, nailing it to his cross:"*

The Amplified version reveals more clearly the meaning of this verse: "having cancelled and blotted out and wiped away the handwriting of the note with its legal decrees and demands, which was in force and stood against us-hostile to us. This note with regulations, decrees and demands He set aside and cleared completely out of our way by nailing it to His Cross."

All the crimes against God, the iniquities, the transgressions, and the sin were nailed to the cross. In the mind of God, a personal writ of execution remains on our cross which reads, "For ye are dead, and your life is hid with Christ in God." (Col. 3:3)

## The Cross forever dooms hostile powers.

Paul explained to the Colossian Christians that the Cross was actually the death blow to the sinister schemes of satan. The hordes of Hell were disarmed by it.

Colosians 2:15 (Amplified Bible)

*[God] disarmed the principalities and powers that were ranged against us and made a bold display and public example of them, in triumphing over them in Him and in it [the cross].*

Every demon came upon Christ when he hung on the Cross. The witnesses who attended His crucifixion saw Him stripped of clothing. His back was lashed by the lector. His brow was pierced from the crown of thorns. His side was split open by a soldier's spear. The people saw nothing but blood. He was unrecognizable due to a merciless beating.

But the scripture reveals that through His suffering and blood, He stripped all of Hell's fiends from Himself.

After stripping them away, He lined them up to expose their defeat. This is the way that conquerors in Bible times paraded their vanquished enemy. Roman history records that when they conquered a kingdom, the defeated country's king, nobles, and officials were chained for the journey to Rome. The conquering general would parade his captives through the gate of the city. Everyone would cheer because the captives were public proof that new territory had been won.

The Apostle Paul's revelation is that Jesus stripped away the powers of darkness from their ruling position. He chained them in a public procession to show that they were conquered for all time. All who catch a vision of the Cross have been enlightened to see our enemies paraded as defeated foes. Alcoholism, drug addiction, promiscuity, hatred, perversion, adultery, pornography, strife, envy, and addiction of every sort are stripped away when we take up the Cross.

The liberated people of God are more than conquerors through Christ. The Seed of the Woman crushed the serpent's head at the Cross.

**The Cross acts as a security fence between the believer and the forces which seek an opportunity to attack.**

The Greek word for cross is "stauros". It means an upright pointed stake. The noun form is used 29 times in the New Testament, and the verb form is found 46 times in the Scriptures. It literally means to "put up posts" as in building a stockade or erecting a fortress. Another form of the word means to "fence around."

The Lord's command to take up the cross means more than crucifying the flesh. The Cross is more than a daily reminder that the believer no longer lives under the curse. The meaning of the Cross goes beyond the writ of execution listing the old sins which have been wiped away. It means more than relief from hostile powers. The Cross is the security fence which keeps the enemy out and the believer safe in the boundaries of righteousness.

The borders of the believer are recognized by only a few. It is a part of the End-Time deception that Christians can flirt with the world and not be hurt. A security fence is needed and the Cross meets the need. In our own strength, we are absolutely vulnerable to devilish forces. But as long as we take up the cross, no plague can come nigh our dwelling. The believer has boundaries, limits, and borders. We are safe inside these boundaries. The Cross does much more than fence us in, it fences evil out. There are places which are off limits to the believer. There are television programs and movies we can't watch. There are thoughts and emotions we can't allow. There are people with which we must not associate. Indulging in these activities means the Cross has been dropped, and our protection has been lost.

Some years ago, Israelis found it necessary to build a $3 million security fence to keep terrorists from gaining access to their country. They were not fencing themselves in, they were fencing their enemies out. The Cross prevents the evil of this present time from invading our life. It is a buffer from the attacks of the flesh and the devil. It keeps the world and all of its corruption out of our life.

**The cross is always pointing forward. It is always focused on the future.**

An old hymn talks about exchanging the old cross for a crown. The day is quickly coming when the Cross bearers will hear the Lord say, "well done." Then we will know the benefits of the cross fully.

**60**

Goshen, the place of divine protection and provision, is populated with people who have taken up the Cross. The enemy recognizes the Cross as the boundary which stops principalities and powers. The cross puts the believer in a place where the devil can not do any permanent damage.

1 John 5:18 (King James Version)

*We know that whosoever is born of God sinneth not; but he that is begotten of God keepeth himself, and that wicked one toucheth him not.*

Until new songs are written about the Cross, we should remember and sing the old ones:

*So I will cherish the old rugged cross,*
*Till my trophies at last I lay down.*
*I will cling to the old rugged cross,*
*And exchange it someday for a crown.*

# CHAPTER 4

# TAKE UP THE YOKE

## (FROM BURDENS TO BLESSINGS)

Matthew 11:29

*Take my yoke upon you, and learn of me; I am meek and lowly in heart: and ye shall find rest unto your souls.*

Joseph's role in bringing his family to Goshen is pivotal in understanding the preparation that Jesus made for our deliverance from present threatening conditions. All Bible scholars agree that Joseph is a type of the Lord Jesus, who was betrayed by his brethren, ill treated, made to suffer, exalted to the right hand of power and eventually reconciled to his own.

When Joseph identified himself to his brothers, the Lord gave him an explanation for the puzzling events of his life:

Genesis 45:7 (King James Version)

*And God sent me before you to preserve you a posterity in the earth, and to save your lives by a great deliverance.*

The word "posterity" should actually be translated "remnant." The remnant of Israel was brought to Goshen in a time of devastating global crisis. The word "remnant" means "those who are left." This term is applicable to real Bible believers in the Last Days who, except for divine intervention, would be on the endangered species list. Despite the present falling away from Biblical absolutes, God will always have a people. Every attempt by demonic powers to extinguish the Upper Room fire is destined to fail.

Our heavenly Joseph, the Lord Jesus, pre-positioned all the resources needed to overcome the danger of these times. The Apostle Peter specifically informed believers living in these days that all temporal and eternal aspects of salvation were ready to be revealed in the Last Time. (1 Peter 1:5) Provision has been made to preserve us as His posterity in the earth.

Those believers who refuse to lose their vital link to the Presence of God are rightly called "the remnant". The remnant refers to the caliber of Christians who survive the present onslaught of iniquity, the prevailing anti-god philosophies, and the tragic departure from righteous living. They are the few that will not compromise. They resist the popular trends and will not hesitate to stand up under the pressure of an evil culture.

Our spiritual Joseph is blazing a path which brings us to a protected place immune to the hazards of this troubled world. He will keep us alive during difficult days. He will spare us from the destruction of perilous times. We, too, have been promised a great deliverance:

Psalms 33:18-19 (King James Version)

*Behold, the eye of the LORD is upon them that fear him, upon them that hope in his mercy; To deliver their soul from death, and to keep them alive in famine."*

It was Joseph who designated Goshen as the temporary residence for Israel. He guaranteed their future with the assurance "there will I nourish thee." (Genesis 45:11 King James Version)

Jesus said the same thing to us when he stated, "Come unto me, all that labour and heavy laden, and I will give you rest." (Matthew 11:28 King James Version)

The "rest" which the Lord offered is not just a description of our Heavenly home. There is a rest which is designed for this side of Eternity. No one can dispute that our time is characterized by unbearable burdens and unsolvable issues. Indescribable stress is rampant and responsible for untold numbers of premature deaths. But Jesus has a word for the struggling and hurting: "come unto me . . . and I will give you rest." It is critical that an anxious and depressed world hear these words again. Just as Goshen was ideal for the needs of Israel, God has provided a perfect plan for all who believe on Him.

Jeremiah 29:11

*For I know the thoughts that I think toward you, saith the LORD, thoughts of peace, and not of evil, to give you an expected end.*

Wagons were provided to transport Jacob and his entire family to Goshen. The instructions were to leave their stuff behind because better things were waiting for them in the appointed place. The wagons were actually a sign to Jacob. It was the arrival of the wagons which made Jacob realize that his transition from famine to plenty would happen in a hurry.

Genesis 45:27 (King James Version)

*And they told him all the words of Joseph, which he had said unto them: and when he saw the wagons which Joseph had sent to carry him, the spirit of Jacob their father revived:*

The worry, depression, grief from the bogus report that his son was dead, stress from depleting supplies, two years of unproductive conditions, and failure from a devastated harvest, evaporated in a moment. The sight of a royal transport brought a surge of energy. An imperial convoy arrived to carry him to a famine-free zone. The wagons were real. It brought a renewed will to live in Jacob. The testimony of the Scripture is that he revived.

A better transport than the regal wagons of Egypt has been sent to carry the believer to the atmosphere, spiritual dimension, and physical reality of a greater place in God. It is a place immune from the world's worsening conditions. Jesus, our Heavenly Joseph, sent the Holy Spirit to carry us from "glory to glory." (2 Corinthians 3:13 King James Version)

The Spirit of God not only convicts the unsaved, He also convinces the believer of greater things to come. He conducts us to spiritual heights where our perspective is totally changed. The Apostle John couldn't have been in a worse place than on the Aegean island called Patmos. Yet, on the Lord's Day, a heavenly transport arrived to take Him to places that transcended time and space. John beheld the triumph over every evil force when he was carried away "in the Spirit". (Revelation 1:10 King James Version) It was the Holy Spirit that transported him "up higher." It was the Holy Spirit that took John to "a great and high mountain" and showed him the capital city of God.

It was the Holy Spirit that snatched Philip from a desert pool where he was baptizing an Ethiopian official and carried him 25 miles to the city of Azotus. (Acts 8:40 King James Version) This transporting ministry of the Holy Spirit happens when God is in a hurry. We are in accelerated mode when the Holy Ghost carries us from "glory to glory."

Jacob saw the royal wagons and knew that the report of Joseph's death was untrue. His grief immediately stopped.

The facts which dominated his life for twenty years changed in an instant. The wagons were the proof that Joseph was alive and the journey out of famine would begin without delay. An encounter with the Holy Spirit will have the same effect on us. Through signs and wonders, the Spirit of God disproves all the theological claims that revival is a thing of the past. Jesus yet lives. Truth has not died. Miracles still happen. Heavenly fire still burns in real worship and praise. The Holy Spirit can take us from nagging doubts to receiving faith in an instant.

He is the royal carrier that lifts us up on eagle's wings. The manifestations of the Spirit transports us to greater glory. The Gifts, demonstrations, miracles, healings, prophecies, and anointing of the Holy Spirit is the supernatural convoy sent to move us out of spiritual and financial famine. Our heavenly Joseph has provided the transports needed to carry us to a modern day Goshen. Such tidings should energize and strengthen us for the journey.

The formula for a revived spirit is spelled out in the Master's instructions: "take up the yoke, and learn of me." Obedience to this command will revive our spirit as Joseph's wagons revived Jacob. It will hasten the trip to divine preservation where sorrow and worry are left behind. Take up the yoke and learn the way to Goshen.

The King James Version of the Scripture translates the Masters words: "take my yoke upon you, and learn **of** me." But in the original Greek text, the words are "take my yoke and learn **from** me." It is from Him that we learn the strategy and receive the ability to overcome.

Jesus is still the pattern, the model, the prototype, and the example. He is the "last Adam" which means that He is the progenitor of a new type of being. The Apostle Paul called us, "new creatures in Christ" to describe our new mode of existence. The miraculous transformation from an offspring of Adam to a child of God cannot be hidden or kept secret.

**67**

The Lord clearly revealed that He never ignites a fire and then conceals it.

Matthew 5:15 (King James Version)

*Neither do men light a candle, and put it under a bushel, but on a candlestick; and it giveth light unto all that are in the house.*

God intends to make it obvious to a lost world that serving Jesus creates a different reality. Isaiah's Endtime prophecy is that the glory and favor of God would be visible on His covenant people. (Isaiah 60:2) Our Savior is also our provider and our protector. He not only redeems the soul of His people, but also enables us to redeem the time. (Col. 4:5) Living in spiritual Goshen means to experience "days of heaven on the earth." (Deuteronomy 11:21 King James Version)

The appearance of these blessings on God's redeemed will have a decided effect on the world. It will provoke many to investigate the reason that the remnant is exempted from the insanity of a collapsing civilization.

Deuteronomy 32:31 (King James Version)

*For their rock is not as our Rock, even our enemies themselves being judges.*

A new reality is shaped by a burning passion to take up the yoke and learn from Him. Their can be only one result:

John 14:12 (King James Version)

*Verily, verily, I say unto you, He that believeth on me, the works that I do shall he do also and greater works than these shall he do; because I go unto my Father.*

Taking up the yoke is an educational directive. It entails a learning experience which informs us about the attributes needed to be healthy, happy, and holy.

The Lord incorporated a yoke in His marvelous invitation to the tired, weary, oppressed, and heavy laden. It was not just any yoke, but His yoke that is offered to alleviate unbearable stress. The unregenerated mind will never be able to comprehend the logic of the Lord's statement. A yoke is indicative of bearing a burden and pulling a load. The question arises, "how can the already overloaded bear anymore burdens?" But remember that His yoke is offered as a replacement, not an addition, to the weights which crush and press upon us. Taking up the yoke is exchanging our burdens for His blessings.

A yoke implies the use of a harness. The Master's words speak of a connection with Him which results in a *great deliverance* from anxiety, stress, and tension. The Lord wants to harness the believer to "peace that passes all understanding", to "joy unspeakable and full of glory," to "victory that overcomes the world", and "to the love of God shed abroad in our heart by the Holy Ghost."

A choice is set before us: either be chained to the trauma of the times, or be harnessed to the promises of the Word.

Dr. Kenneth Wuest was for many years a professor of New Testament Greek at the Moody Bible Institute. He was considered to be one of the foremost Greek scholars in the country. He translated Matthew 11:28 to read: "Come here to me, all who are growing weary to the point of exhaustion, and who have been loaded with burdens and bending beneath their weight, and I alone will cause you to cease from your labor and take away your burdens and thus refresh you with rest."

Jesus taught in everyday illustrations which the common man could understand. All of His teachings are intended to make truth visible by creating an image in our mind. The image which His words convey was a scene well known in Bible times. The Lord was probably in the market place when He spoke of taking up the yoke.

The market place was the hub of activity for towns and cities in ancient times. Carts and carriages were not allowed into the ancient cities of antiquity. The wagons had to be unloaded at the city gates and carried by porters to the marketplace. The poorest of the people were usually commandeered for this task. It was not uncommon to see them weighed down with vast loads of produce tied to their backs.

Crates and baskets which often weighed more than the people who carried them, were strapped to aching backs and shoulders. It was a struggle to get the goods to market. It was an exhausting task to deliver the load. The porters staggered beneath incredible burdens. Their day was spent carrying heavy boxes and baggage. Never was there a moment of relief. Never was their any rest.

Often the loads were so heavy that the porters stopped just long enough to regain a small amount of strength before continuing their long walk. Since they couldn't drop their load, one porter would lean against another in a desperate attempt to steady their buckling legs and catch their breath. Leaning on one another didn't lighten the weight of their burden, but it did give them the opportunity to regain a small respite from their ordeal.

The best that these straining workers could hope for was just a brief moment of relief before grappling with the load of another burden. Jesus was looking at these heavy laden porters leaning on one another when He spoke His timeless promise. He spoke to exhausted and overburdened individuals. He reached out to hopeless, collapsing people and said: 'come unto me all ye that are weary, and heavy laden, and I will give you rest."

It was an invitation to come and lean on Him. Those porters were leaning on people who were just as burdened as themselves. They had the same problems. They shared the same dismal circumstance. They could derive only brief comfort from one another and then return to the weary situation that was draining their life away. But Jesus offered to do more than give temporary relief from the burden. He promised immediate rest to those who leaned on Him and permanent release from crushing weights.

The burden had a purpose. It provided a livelihood. It had to be brought to the marketplace regardless of the struggle. But over time it became too heavy. It is then that Jesus calls out for the overburdened to transfer their load to Him. He said "I alone will cause you to cease from your labors and carry your burdens." It is apparent that the Lord wanted us to know how impossible it is to achieve any worthwhile goal without Him. His strength is needed to finish the task. We can't really make it through any trial or difficulty without Him.

The Greek word "anapauo" was chosen by the Holy Spirit to convey the concept of rest in the original text. It means "to cease from any labor and to recover and recollect strength." These stressful times are taking their toll. Financial stress, family trouble, political upheaval, unexpected reversals, unemployment, economic downturn, are only a few of the factors which have created unparalleled uncertainty. The fear mongers are in full form proclaiming that the worst is yet to come. The consensus is that all will eventually buckle beneath the load.

But there is rest to those who lean on Jesus. Some will lean on their therapist, their accountant, their financial adviser, their favorite politician, a talk-show host, and even their own abilities and talents. All of these temporary supports are limited and finite. Jesus is the only qualified burden-bearer. He offers permanent relief for those who come to Him.

Isaiah 40:29-31 (King James Version)

*He giveth power to the faint; and to them that have no might he increaseth strength.*

*Even the youths shall faint and be weary, and the young men shall utterly fall:*

*But they that wait upon the LORD shall renew their strength; they shall mount up with wings as eagles; they shall run, and not be weary; and they shall walk, and not faint.*

## The Master's call to take up the yoke is specifically given to the bruised and battered.

A short investigation into the word "labour" reveals the meaning of the original word. The Greek word "kopiao", translated "labour" in the King James, is derived from a word that denotes repeated beatings. The word appears several times in the Septuagint, a Greek translation of the Old Testament, to mean tiredness caused by intense battle, groans from the afflicted, and weariness from non-stop toil.

This word is translated "trouble" in Job 5:7: *Yet man is born unto trouble, as the sparks fly upward.* David employed this word to describe his anxiety, exhaustion, and heartbreak: *I am weary with my groaning; all the night make I my bed to swim; I water my couch with my tears.* (Psalm 6:6)

One of the most remarkable occurrences of this word is found in the description of Eleazar's profound battle with the Philistines. Eleazar was one of David's chief warriors. At a time when the entire army of Israel retreated, Eleazar charged into the enemy and slew them until his hand was weary. The enemy just kept coming and Eleazar just kept swinging his sword. This weary soldier stood his ground until the last enemy combatant fell down in defeat. Eleazar

**72**

was worn out by the battle, but "the Lord wrought a great victory that day." (2 Samuel 23:10)

Those who have been beaten up by adverse circumstances and drained by intense trials should be particularly attracted to the words of Jesus. It is in the aftermath of battle that the cost is calculated. There are multitudes of walking wounded that need to heed the Master's call. Jesus is uniquely anointed to "heal the brokenhearted" and "set at liberty them that are bruised."

The time spent in His Presence is a tonic for frayed nerves, exhausted minds, broken hearts, and disturbed spirits. The "beat down" are transformed into the "raised up" by His mighty power.

Many years ago, a wonderful lady in my church experienced a horrendous family tragedy. This precious sister was one of the most Biblically astute Christians I have ever met. She was full of the Holy Ghost and pursued the Lord with a rare passion. She taught the adult Bible class, cultivated a deep prayer life, and was faithful to the House of God. She was a worshipper and a praiser, the highest caliber of believer.

One dark day she received word that turned her world upside down. Law enforcement officers informed her that her eldest son was dead. Further investigation revealed that he had been murdered and that her daughter in law was the prime suspect. The tragic news was more than a jolt to her system, it left her in total shock.

Her boy was a faithful believer and a strong witness to the unsaved, but had become the victim of a senseless killing. Now his children were left fatherless and his mother was bereft of her oldest son.

The investigation went on for days and this precious sister sank deeper and deeper into unbearable grief. She couldn't sleep or eat. Every hour brought endless torment. When the investigators released the body for the funeral, this precious mother was in such anguish that she could barely walk.

Family members had to carry her into the church for the memorial service. Her mind was in such agony that she couldn't make the short trip to the cemetery and had to be taken home. After the committal service, I rushed to her side. Four of her friends were holding her convulsing body on the bed. Another lady was bathing her blood-red face with a wet cloth.

This precious sister was mentally and spiritually strong, but the ordeal had pushed her beyond the limits of endurance. It was apparent that death was in the room ready to exploit the tragedy and claim another victim. But someone else walked into that heartbreaking scene. Jesus, our ever present help, did not abandon her in such a great hour of need. At the direction of the Spirit, I put my hand on her and cried out to the Lord for immediate peace.

Suddenly, the seizures stopped. She wasn't trembling anymore. The incoherent cries of grief came to an immediate end. She raised herself off the bed and said to me, "I'm going to do what David did when he lost his son. I'm getting off this bed. I'm going to wash my face and get something to eat." Her appetite returned and she slept that night.

The tragedy had caused a momentary disconnect from the tangible presence of God. For a few days she was consumed with the grief and injustice of a murdered son. But the yoke was still in place and she was still harnessed to the peace which passes all understanding. Jesus walked through her tormenting emotions and commanded "peace be still."

She was weary and heavy laden, but He took the burden and gave her rest. This dear sister never had a relapse. Instead, she returned to her teaching and became an inspiration to hundreds. She found that His yoke was easy, and His burden was light. The yoke is designed for those who have taken a beating. It is for the ones who have come to the end of their proverbial rope. It is for the wounded and abused.

There are no super-saints in the Body of Christ. Not even the Apostle Paul could escape periodic times of battle fatigue. He admitted to the Corinthian believers:

2 Corinthians 1:8

*For we would not, brethren, have you ignorant of our trouble which came to us in Asia, that we were pressed out of measure, above strength, insomuch that we despaired even of life:*

His missionary work was not all excitement and adventure. He faced intense opposition everywhere he journeyed.

2 Corinthians 7:5

*For, when we were come into Macedonia, our flesh had no rest, but we were troubled on every side; without were fightings, within were fears.*

However, the yoke on this man of God ensured that he would emerge "more than a conqueror". The yoke provided a supernatural peace that he was harnessed to God's omnipotent purpose and power. Paul was repeatedly beaten up, but could always say:

2 Corinthians 4:8-9

*We are troubled on every side, yet not distressed; we are perplexed, but not in despair;*

*Persecuted, but not forsaken; cast down, but not destroyed;*

There will be times when the "battle ready" become the "battle fatigued". There will be times when trouble, stress, and set-back interfere with our God given assignment and attempt to distract our focus from the face of

**75**

Jesus. Disappointment and despair will attempt to detach us from the mighty promises of God. The enemy will fight to hold us captive, but "taking up the yoke" means we have deprived the enemy of any opportunity to hold us back. The yoke is a stable connection to the Mighty God who *daily loadeth us with benefits, even the God of our salvation.* (Ps. 69:19 King James Version)

Our archenemy can only get at us through our stuff. He can only crush us if we refuse to release the burden and give it to Jesus. The believers who are on their way to Goshen have dropped worry, fear, and anxiety. We begin to cross over to the place of divine provision and protection when we cast our cares upon the Lord. (I Peter 5:7)

Joseph's royal directive to Jacob was leave the stuff and board the regal convoy to Goshen. The Lord's divine directive to us is drop the burden, take up the yoke, and experience rest. It is the only way to escape famine. It brings "great deliverance."

# CHAPTER 5

# TAKE UP THE FISH

## (MONEY MIRACLES IN A TIME OF CRISIS)

Matt. 17:27

*Notwithstanding, lest we should offend them, go thou to the sea, and cast an hook, and take up the fish that first cometh up; and when thou hast opened his mouth, thou shalt find a piece of money: that take, and give unto them for me and thee.*

Moving to Goshen became all the more imperative for Jacob and his family as the worldwide famine developed into a full fledged economic collapse. The distress, trouble, and chronic shortages strained the system until the fiscal policies of nations fell apart.

The famine continued to deepen until the money failed.

Genesis 47:15 (King James Version)

*And when money failed in the land of Egypt, and in the land of Canaan, all the Egyptians came unto Joseph, and said, Give us bread: for why should we die in thy presence? for the money faileth.*

The currency and coins were inflated and then devalued. Money lost its purchasing power. Neither savings nor investments could spare people from the severity of the collapse. The world faced an unprecedented crisis. It was far worse than a financial panic or a passing correction in the business cycle. It was beyond an economic downturn. This famine caused a monetary melt-down of epic proportions.

Nothing like it had ever been before. The famine spread through every region of the earth until it became a global crisis. Joseph's inspired leadership enabled Egypt to survive the famine. The Spirit of God made him the only man on earth capable of dealing with the emergency. God taught him crisis management.

But the Lord had something more in mind for the covenant people than merely surviving tough times. Abraham's covenant with God stipulated that his descendants would be overcomers in troubled times, not just survivors. The Lord unequivocally said to Abraham "thy seed shall possess the gate of his enemies". (Genesis 22:17 King James Version)

The Scriptures repeatedly document the fulfillment of this covenant provision. The Hebrews departed the land of their captivity with silver, gold, flocks, herds, spices, and the costly things of the land.


Exodus 12:36 ( King James Version)

*And the LORD gave the people favour in the sight of the Egyptians, so that they lent unto them such things as they required. And they spoiled the Egyptians.*


Haman, the Persian prime minister, was the first ruler who planned genocide against the covenant people. He plotted to exterminate the Jews centuries before demons put the thought into the mind of Hitler and his Nazis. Mordecai was a Persian Jew who understood the provision of Abraham's covenant. He said to queen Esther: "For if thou altogether holdest thy peace at this time, then shall there enlargement and deliverance arise to the Jews from another place." (Esther 4:14 King James Version)

The book of Esther records that the Jews experienced more than deliverance from Haman's wicked plots, thier ordeal resulted in a remarkable enlargement in their standard of living.

Deliverance and enlargement are coupled together for all of God's covenant people in every age. It has always been so. The book of Job is the oldest book in the Bible, but deliverance and enlargement are seen even in this ancient writing. The trouble, trial, and heartbreak that Job endured was really a "set-up" for greater things to come.

Job 42:10 (King James Version)

*And the LORD turned the captivity of Job, when he prayed for his friends: also the LORD gave Job twice as much as he had before.*

The New Covenant in Christ Jesus expands on the promises made to Abraham. The Apostle Paul noted, "And if ye be Christ's, then are ye Abraham's seed, and heirs according to the promise." (Galatians 3:29)

Persecution and attack are inevitable to real believers, but the outcome is assured. When the dust settles from the battle, and we emerge "more than a conqueror" from the conflict, deliverance and enlargement will be the result.

Mark 10:29-30 (King James Version)

*Verily I say unto you, There is no man that hath left house, or brethren, or sisters, or father, or mother, or wife, or children, or lands, for my sake, and the gospel's, But he shall receive an hundredfold now in this time, houses, and brethren, and sisters, and mothers, and children, and lands, with persecutions; and in the world to come eternal life.*

The seed of Abraham is destined to do more than merely make it through a crisis. The covenant people of God are blessed going in to rough times and doubly blessed coming out of it.

The parallel between Joseph's time and our day is just too striking to be ignored. Once again the world is in the grip of a global economic crisis.

All the financial analysis from expert economists agree that the world's currencies are collapsing. The current monetary crisis is devaluing the dollar, the yen, the franc, the mark, and the ruble. Some years ago, the European Union introduced "the euro" as a global currency. Its purpose was to stabilize fluctuating money markets. It was supposed to be immune to the problems of other currencies, but it is so near to collapse, economists believe it will soon fall and be replaced with something else.

The world's present economic condition mirrors Joseph's time. Once again, the money is failing. In that time of dire uncertainty, God sustained His covenant people. They were divinely insulated from a faltering world economy. They thrived in the sheltered place of His protection. The dismal economic disaster did not affect the occupants of Goshen. The northeast section of Egypt was separate from the rest of the country, and exempted from the harsh difficulties which plagued the entire globe.

Goshen functioned by different principles. It had a different environment. Conditions were different there. The Egyptians rejected Goshen because the land was not conducive to their heathen lifestyle. The pagan culture of Egypt hated the pastoral life which was the only life that could be lived there. Only a shepherding people could be comfortable in Goshen, and every shepherd was an abomination to the Egyptians. (Gen. 46:34) The Egyptians would rather deal with the pressure, misery, shortages, headaches, and heartbreaks of famine than experience relief in Goshen.

This attitude of the ancient Egyptians is alive and well in the world today. Through a vital relationship with Jesus, God has provided a spiritual and financial Goshen to bring relief from the horrendous peril of our time. But because a righteous lifestyle is necessary to live in this different environment, the world rejects it.

The Egyptians refused to leave their idolatrous and immoral culture to become a pilgrim "seeking for a city to come whose builder and maker is God." They prided themselves in their accomplishments, construction projects, and advanced civilization. However, their dubious innovations couldn't stop the famine or reverse the destructive trend that dominated their world. They were too prideful to admit that neither their education nor their sophistication could deliver them.

The Egyptian attitude of defiance toward God, even in the face of unprecedented upheaval, is encapsulated in Paul's description of Endtime conditions:

2 Timothy 3:7 (King James Version)

*Ever learning, and never able to come to the knowledge of the truth.*

Romans 1:28 (King James Version)

*And even as they did not like to retain God in their knowledge, God gave them over to a reprobate mind, to do those things which are not convenient;*

Joseph informed his people that Pharaoh would question them about their lifestyle, their occupation, and their way of living. Joseph instructed them to answer forthrightly. In essence, he told them not to be ashamed of what they were. They were not to redefine themselves to be more acceptable to the Egyptians. They were not to seek common ground.

They were to project a confident posture about their distinctive way of life. Joseph knew that if the covenant people were to be preserved in Goshen, then they must maintain their unique difference.

Our heavenly Joseph, the Lord Jesus, has commanded the same response from His covenant people today. When we are attacked by an ungodly culture for Biblical truth and righteous living, it must always be remembered: *Whosoever therefore shall be ashamed of me and of my words in this adulterous and sinful generation; of him also shall the Son of man be ashamed, when he cometh in the glory of his Father with the holy angels.* (Mark 8:38)

There is immense pressure to conform to the politically correct philosophies and notions of our time. Most churches have succumbed to the teaching that all religious roads lead to the same Heaven. Polls and surveys reveal a disturbing trend among professing Christians. There is a definite pattern away from the absolute authority of God's Word. Personal salvation is ignored as the focus of many churches changes to social issues. Demonic Marxism is cloaked in religious trappings under the label of "liberation theology," and the culture that demands tolerance of all beliefs and lifestyles is aggressively intolerant of all Biblical truth.

The movers and shakers of the culture are at war with Biblical Christianity. American Christians are at risk by this ethnic cleansing. Christianity is being hijacked in America by those who advocate a one world religion, and our legal system, instead of defending our rights, is actually reflecting an antichristian bias.

As a result of the political, social, and legal coercion to compromise the Word of God, the believer is under enormous pressure to back away from the cardinal truths of the Scriptures. The world seeks a Christianity without a cross, without the need for repentance, without the certainty of a coming judgment, without a just and holy God, without a divine Savior, without any prohibition or definition of sin, where any practice is permissible, where there is no divine retribution in this life or Eternity, and where good and evil are only relative terms which are redefined by each new generation.

The Christianity which is forced on America is a strange concoction of distorted Scriptural teachings with eastern religions. This new belief system is almost institutionalized. The media, the universities, and a plethora of religious organizations encourage the idea that Allah and Jehovah are the same, Islam is compatible with Christianity, no religion is superior to another, and Eternity is really not all that important.

This deceptive mindset has become so dominant that anyone who holds to the unchanging Word of God is targeted by hostile forces. The enemy's first attempt at destroying the covenant believer is to try to seduce them away from their relationship with Jesus. The social and business advantages of compromising Biblical standards of conduct and endorse the accepted practices of the culture are dangled as bait. The threat of rejection by potential business contacts is pressed on the believer as a reason to accommodate the morays of the times. Career advancement and an elevated social status depend on abandoning Biblical truth in this terminal generation. The world's price for their acceptance is extremely high, but the questionable benefits of compromise are short-lived.

The timeless words of Jesus are all the more poignant in these days:

Mark 8:36-37 (King James Version)

*For what shall it profit a man, if he shall gain the whole world, and lose his own soul?*

*Or what shall a man give in exchange for his soul?*

The enemy has manipulated the national conscience to such a degree that society now regards the worst crimes to be insensitivity, intolerance, and causing offence. If anyone dares believe something different than the accepted politically correct ideology, they are deemed guilty of hate crimes and worthy of punishment.

The faith of Jesus Christ is daily denigrated by politicians and pundits. Our God is mocked by talk-show hosts and late night comedians. Professors turn their classrooms into venues for attacking the Faith. Editors spew their contempt for the Bible in op-ed articles. High School graduates can't speak the Name of Jesus in their commencement exercises and military chaplains are court-martialed if they dare pray in His Name. The real "hate groups" can be seen marching in the streets to strike a blow against marriage and morality. Congress, legislatures, and the courts have chipped away at our inalienable right to worship until precious little of it remains.

The believer is expected to be silent and conform to the present socialization of America. Any defense of the Gospel, or recognition of the country's Christian heritage, or even displaying a symbol of the nation's historic faith is ruled inappropriate, unconstitutional, and offensive. Joseph knew that Pharaoh would probe the possibilities of making Egyptians out of the covenant people. He insisted they tenaciously hold to their testimony and to the pilgrim faith passed down to them from Abraham. Their residence in Goshen depended on their commitment to the covenant.

The answer given to Pharaoh was that Jacob and his family would continue in the faith of their forefathers. Their response to Pharaoh's inquiry opened the way to Goshen. Their bold witness of their unique identity worked in their favor. Pharaoh didn't understand the ways of Jacob, but he respected, appreciated, and favored him with the best of the land.

If we are to enter a protected place where the favor of God shapes our reality, then we must neither conform to the culture nor be timid about our differences with it. We must resist the pressure to back away from the elements of Biblical truth which the culture finds offensive. The old strategy of satan for destroying truth is to make it controversial. If God's people drift from Bible truth because some groups make certain Scriptural demands and teachings controversial, then the old thief has succeeded in his aim at "stealing, killing, and destroying."

The enlightened people of God realize that we can't secure the favor of the Lord if we are cowardly, vacillating, and willing to retreat in the face of opposition. Our apostolic predecessors received a divine boldness that made them depart antagonistic counsels *"rejoicing that they were counted worthy to suffer shame for His Name."* (Acts 5:41 King James Version)

The boldness of First Century believers shook the foundations of society. It intimidated the opposition, but attracted scores to the liberating truth of the Gospel. Their refusal to soft-pedal the Word of God released divine favor which eliminated lack and shortage from their midst.

Acts 4:33 (King James Version)

*And with great power gave the apostles witness of the resurrection of the Lord Jesus: and great grace was upon them all.*

The message coming out of today's Goshen is *"I am not ashamed of the Gospel of Christ: for it is the power of God unto salvation to every one that believeth: to the Jew first, and also to the Greek."* (Romans 1:16)

The Goshen prepared for God's believing children functions by higher principles than the world's system. There are laws of sowing and reaping, giving and receiving, plowing and harvesting that make the financial condition of the redeemed different from the world.

Joseph made it clear to Pharaoh that economic survival depended on the storehouse. The fifth of every harvest was deposited within it. The storehouse is still the key to economic survival. It was God Himself who revealed that financial curses are cancelled when the tithe is brought to the storehouse. (Malachi 3:10)

The tithe is not an option with covenant people. It is a matter of survival. The tithe opens the windows of Heaven in the direction of the tither. The blessings released by the tithe create Goshen-like conditions even in the midst of a global financial meltdown. Obedience to this command places the Lord as the supreme financial counselor. He orchestrates circumstances and situations that bring favor and breakthroughs for His people. He rebukes the devourer. He protects the harvest. He dispatches the heavenly host to bring blessings from unexpected places.

Every believer should ask, "why do I exist on the minimum of God's blessings when He desires the maximum for my life?" Goshen is for believers with different financial priorities than the world. The world attempts to justify any means to achieve a good living, but the believer focuses on a good life. The "good life" to us is an abundant life with resources essential for accomplishing God's divine purpose. The expansion of His Kingdom in human hearts is our reason for living. God withholds nothing from those who align their desires and priorities with His Kingdom:

Matthew 6:33 (King James Version)

*But seek ye first the kingdom of God, and his righteousness; and all these things shall be added unto you.*

Psalms 84:11 (King James Version)

*For the LORD God is a sun and shield: the LORD will give grace and glory: no good thing will he withhold from them that walk uprightly.*

No one gives place to spiritual and financial famine in Goshen. Goshen is the place of abundant supply. It was a miracle place. Around the world wells went dry, rivers stopped flowing, lakes turned to dust, parched ground cracked open from lack of moisture, but none of these maladies happened in Goshen. The entire globe struggled through seven rain-less years, but not in Goshen.

This place of refuge had lush pastures, gushing streams, bubbling fountains, fertile soil and was maintained by the rain of Heaven. The divine provisions in Goshen are preserved in the Word of God to teach believers in these Last Days that we have a heavenly Joseph who promised, ". . . in the world ye shall have tribulation: but be of good cheer; I have overcome the world." (John 16:33 King James Version) The convenant people in Goshen do not deny the tribulations in this present world, but they rejoice that through Jesus, we are exempt from tribulation's destructive capabilities.

Money miracles happen in Goshen.

Matthew records an incident in the Lord's earthly ministry when there was a need for "a piece of money." The temple tax was due, and neither the Lord nor the disciples had the money to pay it. It was a bill that demanded immediate payment. It was a pressing financial need.

After the Lord established that He was really exempted from the tax, He made it clear that He would not make it an issue and offend the Jews. The tax would be paid. The need would be met, but Peter wondered, "where is the money coming from?"

It is the same question that is repeatedly asked by believers with a desire and vision to expand the Kingdom of God. Even the redeemed who are convinced that God wants us blessed wonder, "where is the money coming from?"

Peter was instructed to go fishing for it.

Matthew 17:27 (King James Version)

*Notwithstanding, lest we should offend them, go thou to the sea, and cast an hook, and take up the fish that first cometh up; and when thou hast opened his mouth, thou shalt find a piece of money: that take, and give unto them for me and thee.*

These instructions must have bewildered Peter. After all, he was a professional fisherman. He knew the procedures, the equipment, the methods, and the best times for fishing. He was an expert, but the Lord's instructions were different than accepted norm.

Peter had never before fished in this manner. He was experienced with small, medium, and large catches. At times, he had fished and caught nothing, but Jesus had already proved to Peter who was the better fisherman. There was an occasion when Peter discovered that Jesus could catch more fish with His Word than Peter could with his net. Peter knew that exceptional and miraculous things happened when the Lord spoke the word. (Luke 5:4)

His spoken Word directed a multitude of fish into Peter's empty nets after a night of toil and failure. Success is always the direct result of obedience, so Peter did not argue or debate. He simply got his hook and line and headed to the sea.

This fishing expedition was not for fish, but for a piece of money. Peter was not fishing by experience or depending on his many years of accumulated knowledge. He was fishing by revelation. The revelation of the Word said there is a fish in the sea with a piece of money in his mouth, so Peter positioned himself to be at the right place to catch a miracle.

More than a hook was dropped in the water. Along with that hook was Peter's faith and expectation. No one knows how long Peter waited for the fish to swallow the hook. All we know is that Peter patiently waited for the miracle, and the miracle happened just like Jesus said.

There is a specific type of fish in the Sea of Galilee which is called Saint Peter's fish. This species of fish lives in deep water and strikes at bright objects. At an earlier time, someone carelessly dropped a coin into the water and a fish swallowed it. It was swimming around in the sea until Peter's hook caught its attention. The reflection of the hook in the clear water of the blue Galilee mesmerized the fish and it swam directly toward the hook.

Peter was on the surface, waiting for the tug on the line. Everything about this financial miracle happened beneath the surface. Peter had no idea about the activity beneath the waves. He just kept holding the line. God's people who are in need of a financial miracle need to understand that somewhere beneath the surface, unknown to us, a miracle is coming from deep water and swimming in our direction.

Money miracles require that we do not look at the things which are seen, but at the things which are not seen. (2 Corinthians 4:18 King James Version) More is happening below the surface than we know. The faith which the believer inserts into the situation causes hidden resources beyond our reach to swim in our direction.

A better job, better investments, and a financial breakthrough is moving toward those who continue to keep their hook of faith in the water and firmly hold the line of expectation. Long before the financial need developed, the Lord had the fish in the right place. The fish could only swallow the hook that Peter put in the water. There wasn't even a remote possibility that someone else would hook that fish.

The faithful covenant believer need only use their faith to hook a miracle. The answer is swimming somewhere in our situation right now. The piece of money needed to pay the debt will shortly fasten to the line. Expect the tug on the line to come at any moment.

The fishing has never been better than it is today in Goshen.

# CHAPTER 6

# THEY SHALL TAKE UP SERPENTS

## (OVERCOMING DEMONIC OPPOSITION)

Mark 16:18

*They shall take up serpents; and if they drink any deadly thing, it shall not hurt them; they shall lay hands on the sick, and they shall recover.*

Goshen is not a fantasy land where people live in denial and pretend that no problem or enemy exists. It is a spiritual environment that transforms the vicinity around the believer into a plague-free zone. The surroundings of any person who is truly in covenant with God can be transformed into a Goshen-like environment.

Goshen is the representation of "the secret place" lauded by the Psalmist. It is a close relationship with Jesus which insulates the believer from the destructive conditions of a collapsing world. It is dwelling in "the shadow of the Most High" where no plague can come near. It is living an exceptional life of overcoming victory and establishing boundaries that no demon can violate.

Goshen is a protected region where its occupants are nourished by the highest authority. It is a sector of reality that is off-limits to devilish principalities and powers. It is a spiritual dimension where enemy strongholds have been demolished and spanned by an open heaven devoid of all nefarious spirits. It is where the "prince of the power of the air" cannot function.

The five miraculous signs that Jesus said would follow the believer characterize the occupants of the Last Day Goshen:

Mark 16:17-18 (King James Version)

*And these signs shall follow them that believe; In my name shall they cast out devils; they shall speak with new tongues;*

*They shall take up serpents; and if they drink any deadly thing, it shall not hurt them; they shall lay hands on the sick, and they shall recover.*

These signs are attesting miracles. These manifestations of divine deliverance should never be regarded as empty expressions of supernatural power. The Lord designed these works of the Holy Spirit to carry an unmistakable message of eternal superiority over all the machinations of the devil.

Mark's Gospel concludes with a declaration that the believer has been endued with new power, new tongues, new protections, and new ministries to expel the enemy and all his agents from our territory. The Greek word "follow" means to "be always present; to attend one wherever he goes; to follow faithfully; a standard and a rule". No serious student of the Scripture can read this passage without knowing that God intends for these miracles to be the norm for Bible Christians.

For many years, seminary professors and leaders of dead denominations have attempted to extract this portion of God's Word from the Bible. The critics have invented dozens of theories to discredit this passage, but it still remains a beacon of hope to a dying world. Certain self-styled Bible scholars are quick to emphasis that this portion of Mark's Gospel does not appear in the two oldest Greek manuscripts. However, if anyone dares investigate the matter, it will be learned that of the 618 ancient Greek manuscripts in existence, only two have omitted the final verses of Mark's Gospel.

The New Testament was first translated in Syriac in 150 A.D. and it contains this passage. Jerome in 382 A.D. had access to the original manuscripts and he included this passage in his Latin version of the New Testament. There are about 100 ancient Christian writers who wrote before the oldest surviving Greek manuscripts. All their writings refer to this passage in Mark. The comment about this passage in the Angus Bible Handbook says, "the overwhelming mass of manuscripts, versions, and Apostolic Fathers are in favor of these verses" as part of the original Gospel of Mark. We can trust them to be the very words of Jesus.

But the modernists are embarrassed by these miraculous signs. Since the very beginning, the devil has incessantly attempted to remove all supernatural elements from the Word of God. It has always been the strategy of our arch-enemy to dilute the Scriptures into a lifeless and powerless piece of religious literature. There is a devilish plot to deceive people into regarding the Word of God as nothing more than Hebrew legend or Christian myth. The enemy is behind all the present efforts to interpret the Scripture as allegory and mere moralistic fables.

However, the Bible remains the timeless, changeless, immutable, and infallible Word of Almighty God. These words of the Master in Mark's Gospel can never be erased. Mark concludes his narrative by informing believers that power is consistently released to us in the Name of Jesus. These five things were not isolated incidences, but comprised the standard for Spirit-filled believers: "they went forth, and preached everywhere, the Lord working with them, and confirming the Word with signs following. "Amen" (Mark 16:20)

The statement that "the Lord worked with them" means Jesus put forth power as a partner in labor. He supplied and dispatched the supernatural ability to cast out devils, speak with new tongues, take up serpents, protect from poison, and secure the recovery of the sick through laying on of hands.

**It should be noted that God has a specific purpose in depositing power in the believer to take up serpents.**

This sign is not an invitation to handle snakes. Only the most disingenuous or ignorant person could read this meaning into the text. Jesus is not referring to a side show of exhibiting mastery over snakes like the snake charmers which abounded in pagan cultures. All five of these signs refer to victory over hostile demonic forces. The words of Jesus must not be construed to refer to the danger of venomous reptiles, but to the more profound threat of devilish forces that strike at humanity with sin and death.

The Master's description of taking up serpents is actually a reference to demonstrating power over satanic enemies. Since the Garden of Eden, satan chose the serpent to be his mascot. From Genesis to Revelation, the Word of God refers to the Evil One as "that old serpent, the dragon, the devil, and satan." It was the devil in the serpent that beguiled Eve. In Isaiah 27:1, God promised to slay the crooked, piercing serpent.

The crucial battle which transpires midway into the coming seven years of Tribulation pits the archangel Michael and the host of heaven against the old serpent and his fallen compatriots. (Revelation 12:7) The old serpent is a fitting symbol of our enemy who will one day be chained and cast into the bottomless pit.

The Greek word translated "take up" in our English Bibles means "to remove, to take away, to destroy, to put away, and do away with." This is the treatment the empowered believer gives to demonic forces which strike at us with their venom of destruction. The Lord releases His power through the believer to remove and put away the old serpent:

Luke 10:18-19 (King James Version)

*And he said unto them, I beheld Satan as light-ning fall from heaven.*

*Behold, I give unto you power to tread on serpents and scorpions, and over all the power of the enemy: and nothing shall by any means hurt you.*

The ancient Israelite priests found it necessary to peri-odically cleanse the Temple from the debris brought into it by the massive crowds. They had to do more than remove the ashes from the altar of sacrifice and wash the furnish-ings. The atmosphere of the Temple needed to be cleansed as well. They accomplished their task by walking through the House of God quoting Psalm 91. They believed that ver-bally releasing the Word of God into the air drove out every evil influence. Psalm 91 became known as "The Psalm that makes the demons flee."

Psalm 91 retains its mighty power today. The ability to crush the serpent under our feet is released when the thir-teenth verse is spoken: *Thou shalt tread upon the lion and adder: the young lion and the dragon shalt thou trample under feet.*

The serpent always represents those things which are hostile to God. There are three occasions in the Gospels which refer to Pharisees and hypocrites as "a generation of vipers." The motive of these dead religionists was to destroy the new life which Jesus offered a hurting, suffering, and sinful humanity. John the Baptist didn't mince words when he said to the religious hierarchy, "O generation of vipers, who has warned you to flee from the wrath to come."

The Lord once singled out a group of blasphemers and said, "O generation of vipers, how can ye, being evil, speak good things? For out of the abundance of the heart the mouth speaketh." Those people had a serpent in their heart.

Toward the end of the Master's earthly ministry, He indicted the Pharisees again as "hypocrites, ye serpents, ye generation of vipers, how can ye escape the damnation of hell?" (Matthew 23:33) The believers in these Last Days are opposed by a modern generation of vipers who spew out poisonous, damning, and destructive words as readily as a snake injects venom into its victim. There is a vast cadre of hateful voices which seek to tear down our faith with their maniacal statements.

In addition to the demon possessed groups that scream against us, the enemy strategically places talebearers in our path. Solomon noted: "The words of a talebearer are as wounds, and they go down into the innermost parts of the belly." (Proverbs 18:8)

The Scripture notes that satan has the power to transform some people into human vipers and use their tongue in releasing as much death as a cobra's fangs.

Job 20:16 (King James Version)

*He shall suck the poison of asps: the viper's tongue shall slay him.*

A viper is a species of snake that hisses every time it inhales and exhales. It is called the horned viper because of two protruding tissues at the top of its head. It burrows itself in the sand with only its eyes and horns sticking out and ambushes its prey. It lies flat and glares at its intended victim, but it is not very successful. The viper fails because most creatures can smell it and sniff out its hiding place. The viper emits an odor that warns potential victims that they are walking into an ambush.

Inherent in the believer is the ability to sense those times and places where satan has burrowed himself in specific situations and intends to strike. One of the reasons that every believer must be filled with the Holy Spirit is because He acts as our early warning system. (John 16:13) The

Scripture admonishes us to "prove all things; hold fast that which is good. Abstain from all appearance of evil." (I Thessalonians 5:21) God has put in the church the "discerning of spirits" to expose the devices, traps, and deceptions of the enemy. Defeat and destruction can be avoided in these Last Days if we learn to listen to the Holy Ghost.

There are certain characteristics of satan which can't be hid. Any situation that is compromising, lewd, suggestive, provocative, dishonest, or covetous is a trap where the old serpent is planning an ambush. Anything that has to be covered up by a lie has a snake lurking about it. The devil has a foul odor of unbelief, disobedience, fear, and sensuality. If we ever find ourselves in an atmosphere befouled with the distinctive stench of satan, be prepared to "resist the devil, and he will flee."

Romans 16:20 (King James Version)

*And the God of peace shall bruise Satan under your feet shortly. The grace of our Lord Jesus Christ be with you. Amen.*

Although there are dozens of different species of snakes, the Word of God speaks of only three: the adder, the viper, and the python. The asp is the same species as the adder and is thought to be the modern cobra. It blinds its victim by spitting a stinging solution into their eyes. Then it slowly slithers near its victim and sinks its fangs deep into its prey. The venom attacks the nervous system causing muscular paralysis. It's a deadly creature, and a fitting symbol of demons that blind and paralyze.

Multitudes today are in danger of being fatally bitten by the old serpent because of their appalling spiritual blindness. We are literally inundated with prophetic signs which scream to a lost world and a sleeping church that Jesus is coming soon. But the venom of indifference is paralyzing

**97**

thousands who are losing all feeling for the things of God. The poison of apathy is numbing spiritual muscles. Prayer, praise, worship, and service have been curtailed and substituted with carnal pursuits.

The asp was the preferred snake of Pharaoh's magicians. The Scripture records that in the first encounter between Moses and Pharaoh, Moses threw down his rod and it became a serpent. The serpent had a special meaning in Egyptian society and religion. A metal serpent adorned the headband of Pharaoh to create fear in his subjects. Egyptians kept snakes in their temples as an object of worship. Serpents were associated with the realm of the dead. They would appear in their dreams and speak to them.

Pharaoh called his magicians, who were experienced snake charmers, to counter Moses. It was a common trick among these enchanters to hypnotize snakes into a stiff position so they would take on the appearance of a staff. Then at the right moment, the charmers would drop the snake to the ground where it looked as though the stick turned into a serpent.

However, something unplanned and unprecedented happened in Pharaoh's court when Moses entered to demand the release of God's people. Pharaoh was confident that he could embarrass Moses by equaling a miracle of God with a magician's trick. The hoax worked flawlessly until Moses' rod swallowed up the magician's serpents. The serpents were instruments of death. Moses' rod was an instrument of deliverance and life. Pharaoh's court was thrown into consternation when God's rod of divine power swallowed up satan's serpents of death.

The power to take up serpents is the ability to defeat the enemy on his own ground. According to the Scriptures, the yielded and obedient believer is infused with divine authority to bring holy chaos to the present order of things. The New Testament church turned their world upside down. We can do no less. Strongholds will soon be attacked and demolished. Multitudes held captive by the sinful status quo will soon be freed. The Greater One isn't finished yet. Goshen is really a staging ground for the promised greater glory, and once the remnant has been fully mobilized, this nation will again shake with the mighty presence of God.

The viper was the serpent that gave no warning, struck without notice, and crawled into places where no one would suspect a serpent was hiding. It hid where people were accustomed to gather. It searched for well worn paths and hid in the sand. It attacked horses, camels, donkeys, and any other creature that carried riders travelling down the road.

Jacob observed the intent of the adder in his prophecy about Dan:

Genesis 49:17 (King James Version)

*Dan shall be a serpent by the way, an adder in the path, that biteth the horse heels, so that his rider shall fall backward.*

The adder lurked in strategic places to prevent people from arriving at their destination. People rode rather than walked when they were in a hurry, but the adder was waiting to strike and make the rider fall backward. The adder is in the way to throw the believer backward from his purpose, call, and divine destiny. Unlike the venom of Pharaoh's cobras, the venom of the adder attacked the circulatory system. It went directly to the heart. The believer must be diligent concerning the affections and emotions of the heart lest the adder in the path destroy our love for God.

Proverbs 4:23 (King James Version)

*Keep thy heart with all diligence; for out of it are the issues of life.*

Every observer of prophecy realizes that God is accelerating the times. The Apostle Paul made it clear that the world would reach a moment in time when God *"will finish the work, and cut it short in righteousness: because a short work will the Lord make upon the earth."* Romans 9:28

In the Lord's discussion of Endtime events, He spoke of shortening the days. (Matthew 24:22) The lull in prophetic events is over. Israel, Russia, Iran, Europe, China, Saudi Arabia, the Palestinians, and Muslim nations are taking their Endtime positions. The prophesied one world economy, global government, and amalgamated religion of antichrist is emerging. Jerusalem has become the contentious issue hamstringing peace negotiations, just as the prophet foretold. (Zechariah 12:2) The apostate church predicted to dominate the Last Days is gaining momentum. Events are rapidly moving the world to the prophesied seven years of Tribulation and propelling the glorious church to its meeting with Jesus in the air.

However, the Body of Christ in this nation has not reached its spiritual destination. There is one more revival, one more awakening, one more outpouring yet to come. The prophet Isaiah spoke of the covenant people transported on "swift beasts" to fulfill God's divine purpose. (Isaiah 66:20)

We are on the road to revival, but the adder is determined to strike and cause us to fall backward. The believer's authority to take up serpents gives us the ability to clear the path of hidden dangers like the military's mine sweepers remove hidden explosives. We can't fall backward at this late date. The enemy must not be permitted to gain an advantage over us. There is no time to slow down.


Jeremiah 1:12 (King James Version)

*Then said the LORD unto me, Thou hast well seen: for I will hasten my word to perform it.*

Habakkuk 2:3 (King James Version)

*For the vision is yet for an appointed time, but at the end it shall speak, and not lie: though it tarry, wait for it; because it will surely come, it will not tarry.*

The serpents that position themselves to hinder and block our progress must be taken out of the way. A serpent attempted to keep the Apostle Paul from fulfilling his assignment at Rome. Paul was traveling as a prisoner aboard a ship bound for the imperial city when a storm threatened to destroy them. The ship broke apart from the fierce winds and waves, but everyone that held to a board or a piece of the torn ship arrived safely at land. The rain poured down upon the shipwrecked survivors as they washed ashore on the island of Melita. The temperature dropped and the cold set in.

While Paul gathered sticks to fuel the fire, he inadvertently picked up a bundle were a viper was hiding. The snake remained hidden until it hit the fire. The snake could not stand the heat and responded to the fire by latching on to Paul's hand. Fire always disturbs snakes. The Pentecostal fire which came on the 120 in the Upper Room agitates every demonic force wherever it falls. The mighty baptism in the Holy Ghost is the only demon repellant available. The promised power creates a barrier that is impervious to the foul spirits that seek our hurt.

The heathen people watched with bated breath, expecting Paul to swell and suddenly fall dead. But instead, Paul "shook off the beast into the fire, and felt no harm". The original opinion of these heathen people was that Paul must be a criminal whose misdeeds demanded death for some heinous act, but when he shook off the viper into the fire, they changed their minds.

It must be recognized that today many people are misinformed and indoctrinated against God's covenant redeemed. The unflattering opinion of true Bible believers has been molded in the masses by an antagonistic media that seeks to eliminate all Christian influences. However, the present search for answers to these stressful times has left multitudes bewildered and yearning for truth. When they see real Spirit-filled believers shake off the trouble, worry, fear, and torment which has proved so deadly and pervasive in our generation, they will change their minds.

It may take some searching, but there are places where Holy Ghost fires still burns. It is in those uncompromising churches, ablaze with heavenly anointing, that hidden things which block answers to prayer come to the surface. It is in the atmosphere of total worship, praise, and ministry, that serpents are shaken off and their intended victims feel no harm.

The third species of serpents mentioned in the Scriptures is the python. This species is especially associated with demonic attempts at manipulating and distorting future events to human beings. The Hebrew and Greek word translated "divination" actually means a python spirit.

The ancient world was filled with temples where serpents were said to speak messages to selected individuals. The Babylonians kept snakes in their temples for such purposes. The symbol of the Babylonian god, Bel, was a snake-dragon. The Greeks used snakes to make connection to their principle deity, Zeus. There was a large temple erected to the Greek idol Askelpios in the ancient city of Pergamos. The idol was a wreathed serpent and was identified as "satan's seat." (Revelation 2:13)

The python spirit emitted a hypnotic power over its victims and captivated them in a trance-like state. The unsuspecting prey bowed to its mesmerizing suggestions. The Biblical directive in Leviticus 19:26 forbids the use of "enchantments" and the passage literally means "do not hold conversations with serpents."

The python's technique is to wrap itself around its prey and crush its victims. Then it unlocks it jaws and swallows the carcass. The python is a fitting image of a controlling habit which winds itself around an individual, progressively seizing more of life until it suffocates and crushes them. Addictions act like a python, squeezing all emotions and life from the soul. Sinful obsessions is actually a monster that swallows a person whole.

There is an episode recorded in Acts 16:16 where the python spirit wrapped itself around a young girl. This girl was possessed by a spirit of divination and intended to confuse the Philippian people by indentifying herself with the evangelistic ministry of Paul and Silas. For many days, this woman interrupted the apostles' mission by drawing attention to herself.

Paul became grieved over the bondage of this poor girl and the spirit which drove her to continually disrupt the ministry of the Word. The signs of the believer operated in him to deliver this poor girl from the grip of a demon spirit which manipulated her like a puppet. He said to the spirit, "I command thee in the Name of Jesus Christ to come out of her. And he came out the same hour."

The python spirit unwrapped itself from her mind, soul, and body. She was free because Paul didn't hesitate to activate the delivering power of the Holy Spirit by commanding the demon to leave. It was a one sided conversation. When the spirit of divination heard the Name of Jesus, he had no choice but to release the suffocating coils from his victim and slither away.

Taking up serpents is spiritual warfare against the powers of darkness. It is a ministry of deliverance which sets the captive free. It is a sign following the believer. The thousands of imprisoned souls whose minds are controlled by demon powers can be freed when the serpent is forced to unwind itself from their life. The authority to destroy the works of the devil has been delegated to Spirit filled believers. Through the Name of Jesus we can remove, destroy, and put away the old serpent.

It is imperative that the child of God understand that we cannot co-exist with snakes. The wicked practices, thoughts, attitudes, and pleasures of a condemned world have venomous fangs that kill. The clear command of Scripture is *"Neither give place to the devil."* (Ephesians 4:27)

There is a place in God where the Holy Spirit is a "force field" holding back the powers of satan. The Apostle Paul wrote of deliverance from enemy control, and translation to heavenly territory made possible through the blood of Jesus.

Colossians 1:13-14 (King James Version)

*Who hath delivered us from the power of darkness, and hath translated us into the kingdom of his dear Son: In whom we have redemption through his blood, even the forgiveness of sins:*

Jacob discovered that he could not enter Goshen without a sacrifice. The blood on the altar made it possible to journey from famine to plenty. It eliminated the fear of the unknown so that he could move to greater things.

Genesis 46:1 (King James Version)

*And Israel took his journey with all that he had, and came to Beer-sheba, and offered sacrifices unto the God of his father Isaac. . . and they came to the land of Goshen. (Gen. 46:28)*

The blood of Jesus constitutes the border surrounding the believer in the safe haven of a Goshen-like environment. It is a boundary that demons can't cross. The power of the blood, the authority of His Name, the anointing of the Spirit, and the promise of His Word provide effective energy in removing, destroying, and putting away all serpents.

The snakes of Egypt can't slither their way into Goshen. It is the place of protection and divine provision. It is time to travel where the agents of the curse can't enter.

# CHAPTER 7

# THE WAGONS ARE READY

Goshen is God's pictorial album of Endtime conditions for remnant believers. It reveals a dimension of spiritual reality close to Jesus where the redeemed enjoy the full benefits of divine kinship. Just as the privileges and prerogatives of Joseph's high office were directed toward his family, the believer has been elevated to the status of an heir and joint heir with Christ.

Just as Joseph allocated resources and provisions to sustain his people, the Lord Jesus has given us all things that pertain to life and godliness. Just as Joseph orchestrated events to save the Hebrews with a "great deliverance", Jesus is coordinating conditions that make all things work together for the good of them that love the Lord and are called according to His purpose.

Just as Joseph sent a royal convoy to transport grieving Jacob out of famine, our Master sent the Holy Spirit to carry us from lack and want to continual abundance. Just as Goshen was ideally suited to meet Jacob's needs, our God is creating the circumstances which meet the needs of His covenant people according to His riches in Glory.

A caravan of pack mules laden with costly things from Egypt was first sent to convince Jacob that provisions were waiting for him in Goshen. The wagons arrived to expedite his rescue from famine and accelerate the departure from unbearable conditions.

The wagons were Jacob's way of escape.

The current crisis, which threatens the world's financial and economic stability, would be a cause of concern for the believer if were not for the fact that our heavenly Joseph, the Lord Jesus, has provided a way of our escape. His caravan of spiritual and material blessings daily supports us in these shaking times, but something better is on the way. The Spirit of God, like a divine transport, is moving through the earth right now to carry remnant believers to Goshen-like conditions. He is ready to begin our journey of faith to a place of provision and protection as we await our ultimate exodus from this judgment bound world.

1 Corinthians 10:13 (King James Version)

*There hath no temptation taken you but such as is common to man: but God is faithful, who will not suffer you to be tempted above that ye are able; but will with the temptation also make a way to escape, that ye may be able to bear it.*

Goshen was an exceptional place. It was exempted from the dearth which enveloped the entire world. A divine exemption from deteriorating earthly conditions is issued when believers appropriate faith in the mighty promises of God. Living in Goshen means an environment where we are blessed in a cursed world, have peace in the midst of turmoil, enjoy provisions at a time of appalling shortages, experience prosperity in a world of poverty, and encounter success in a climate of failure.

The remnant believer is destined to be the exception of current trends.

Goshen is a place of divine favor insulating the covenant people from the danger of perilous times. It is where the

Presence of the Lord becomes a wall of protection forbidding any access to demon powers. Goshen is off limits to the rulers of the darkness of this world.

Consider a few of the provisions which give us a pass through troubled times:

### 1. Isaiah 43:2

*When thou passest through the waters, I will be with thee; and through the rivers, they shall not overflow thee: when thou walkest through the fire, thou shalt not be burned; neither shall the flame kindle upon thee.*

### 2. Jeremiah 17:7-8

*Blessed is the man that trusteth in the LORD, and whose hope the LORD is.*

*For he shall be as a tree planted by the waters, and that spreadeth out her roots by the river, and **shall not see when heat cometh**, but her leaf shall be green; and shall not be careful in the year of drought, neither shall cease from yielding fruit.*

### 3. 1 John 5:18

*We know that whosoever is born of God sinneth not; but he that is begotten of God keepeth himself, and **that wicked one toucheth him not**.*

### 4. Luke 10:19

*Behold, I give unto you power to tread on serpents and scorpions, and over all the power of the enemy: and **nothing shall by any means hurt you**.*

**107**

Famine was a condition of extreme shortages. It meant hardship, fear, uncertainty, failure, and eventual death. It meant that hunger and thirst ruled the day.

Joseph grasped the urgency of moving Jacob quickly out of famine, so the royal wagons were sent to fetch him. The archenemy was using famine to destroy Abraham's heritage. The severity of conditions in Canaan demanded that the seed of Abraham be transported to Goshen in a hurry. Time was of the essence, and if satan's plan against God's people were to be overturned, then something had to be done speedily.

The same urgency exists today when so many of God's people are close to the breaking point. Adversity, unexpected reversals, difficulties, and trouble of every description drain away our spiritual, mental, emotional, and financial resources. The pressure and stress of the times is creating a real famine for multitudes.

The arrival of wagons from Goshen was a sign to Jacob convincing him that deliverance had come. The Holy Spirit uses the Word of God for the same purpose. The Scripture can transport the believer to better conditions. The promises of the Lord are powerful when they are released into our situation. The mighty Word of God can reshape our reality. Our Heavenly Joseph has a sent a word to carry us out of famine:

Job 5:20 (King James Version)

*In famine he shall redeem thee from death: and in war from the power of the sword.*

Job 5:22 (King James Version)

*At destruction and famine thou shalt laugh: neither shalt thou be afraid of the beasts of the earth.*

Ps 33:18-19 (King James Version)

*Behold, the eye of the LORD is upon them that fear him, upon them that hope in his mercy; To deliver their soul from death, and to keep them alive in famine.*

Ps 37:18-19 (King James Version)

*The LORD knoweth the days of the upright: and their inheritance shall be for ever.*

*They shall not be ashamed in the evil time: and in the days of famine they shall be satisfied.*

Romans 8:35-37 (King James Version)

*Who shall separate us from the love of Christ? shall tribulation, or distress, or persecution, or famine, or nakedness, or peril, or sword?*

*As it is written, For thy sake we are killed all the day long; we are accounted as sheep for the slaughter.*

*Nay, in all these things we are more than conquerors through him that loved us.*

The believer can ride these Scriptures to better days just as Jacob rode the wagons to Goshen. These promises are signs to people who are subsisting in famine-like conditions. The imperial wagons contained provisions needed to get Jacob and his family to Goshen, and the mighty Word of God supplies the faith which sustains us on our journey to the breakthrough. THE REMNANT BELIEVER MUST GET READY TO RIDE.

Faith was needed for Jacob to leave the famine. Strength was needed to make the journey to Goshen. The old patriarch was bereft of both strength and faith until he saw the wagons. The wagons brought a revelation which infused Jacob with fresh faith and new strength.

The narrative in Genesis reveals that neither the report of his sons nor the caravan of loaded pack mules sparked faith in Jacob's heart. It was not until he saw the wagons sent to carry him to Goshen that "the spirit of Jacob their father revived."

There was a revelation in the wagons.

The Hebrew word "revived" describes the affect that the regal convoy had on Jacob. It means that he recovered, was restored, and made alive. The sight of royal transportation made the "old" Jacob live again.

The Jacob that could tenaciously hold on to God and say, "I will not let you go until you bless me" came back to life. The Jacob that could peer into the spirit realm and behold the angels ascending and descending upon the heavenly staircase revived. The spirit of the man who could place a marker at Heaven's Gate and partner with God for future exploits, returned and lived once more.

There had to be a powerful revelation in the wagon to make a man bound with 20 years of grief suddenly rise to a new level of faith.

Something among the gifts and provisions persuaded Jacob that Joseph was alive. The Scriptures do not reveal the specific item which changed Jacob's heart, but it is possible to surmise the mysterious something that stirred Jacob's faith. Joseph was the closet to his father of all Jacob's twelve sons. He was the oldest son of his beloved Rachel. Jacob decided that Joseph would be given the right of the first born, and designated him as the future leader of the clan by giving him a specially made coat.

The Scriptures call it a "coat of many colors." The coat was torn from Joseph and daubed with goat's blood to give credence to the lie that he had been killed by wild animals.

Neither Jacob nor Joseph ever forgot the colors of that coat. Twenty years of Joseph's struggle in Egypt, and twenty years of Jacob's sorrow in Canaan, could not blur the memory of those colors. The colors of the coat united Jacob and Joseph in a common purpose. It was the insignia of closeness, fellowship, and communion between father and son. The colors on the coat were more than decoration. The colors indicated hope, authority, and faith in a holy covenant that would endure the test of time and span the generations. The Scriptural text details that Joseph distributed garments to each of his brothers, and five changes of raiment were given to Benjamin before they left Egypt on the return trip to Canaan.

There were robes and garments in the royal wagons, and it is altogether possible, that a coat of many colors, like the one Joseph was wearing when Jacob saw him last, was lying among them. This is entirely conjecture, but it is certain that something in the wagon brought a personal revelation to Jacob. Something made him believe. Something ended his grieving and started him believing again.

It had to be personal. It had to be a private sign from Joseph. It made Jacob shout, "Joseph my son is yet alive: I will go and see him before I die."

The Spirit of God desires to minister to every overwhelmed believer. Perhaps years of sorrow have dominated the time and created a personal famine which dried up all joy and peace. If only those believers had an ear to hear what the Spirit is now saying to the church. The remnant believers must hear the divine announcement that heavenly transports have arrived to take us to greater things.

Just as Jacob needed a revelation to leave his sorrowful surroundings, a revelation from the Holy Spirit is needed to activate the faith which alters our present circumstances. It may happen during a time of private devotions, or when effectual fervent prayer boils out of our soul, or when we are engaged in intense praise, or bowed before the Lord in total worship. But at some moment of drawing near to His Presence, a visitation of the Holy Spirit will come with an intimate sign indicating our breakthrough has arrived.

The manifestations of the Spirit bring exhortation, edification, and comfort. Times of intimacy with Him bring divine assurance that God has not departed from His original plan for our life. Even though trouble and sorrow may have delayed the promise, nothing can ever cancel it out.

Philippians 1:6 (King James Version)

*Being confident of this very thing, that he which hath begun a good work in you will perform it until the day of Jesus Christ:*

If the royal transports are inspected, a personal sign from the Lord will be discovered. Just as the colors of Joseph's coat would always stand for authority, position, and inheritance, the truth of God's Word will never change from its original meaning. The Holy Spirit by dreams, visions, prophecies, promises, sermons, testimonies, songs, prayer, tracts, books, and in a multitude of other methods is ministering and confirming the unchanging Word of God in personal and intimate ways.

The colors of the coat had meaning to just Jacob and Joseph. God knows what manifestation of His Spirit will spark faith in all of us. The caravan of anointed ministry is just now arriving to a spiritually famine-ridden America. There is a miracle coming that is tailor-made for every believer who dares to believe.

The wagons are here and ready to carry us to Goshen. It is time to hasten from famine to divine provisions prepared for us in these Last Days. Examine the divine carriers and discover that Jesus still lives and reigns. Revival is in the wagon. Our heavenly Joseph has sent something in His royal transports that will make your spirit revive, live, and rejoice again. Enjoy the ride to greener pastures and an abundant supply.

Welcome to Goshen!

9 780881 442069